Working with Embodiment in Supervision

Working with Embodiment in Supervision: A systemic approach offers a number of approaches to working with the body in therapy and counselling supervision. The authors are all experienced supervisors of clinical practice.

The book is divided into two parts. Part I addresses how power and difference are embodied, exploring implications for the supervisory process. Part II offers supervisees and supervisors practices for using our bodies with intention in supervision, working with physical sensation, emotion and bodily movement and expression. The book introduces a repertoire of innovative practices for supervisors to reflect on, talk about and work with embodiment in supervisory practice and includes exercises and detailed guides to assist readers in using the practices in their own work.

Working with Embodiment in Supervision will be of use for practitioners (both supervisors and supervisees) involved in supervision of clinical practice, as well as trainers and trainees engaged in supervision training. It should also be of interest to those who want to address embodiment in mental health, psychology, psychotherapy and counselling practice.

Jo Bownas is a consultant systemic psychotherapist and supervisor working within the NHS. She provides supervision and consultation to therapists and other practitioners working in the National Health Service, in social care, and in independent practice.

Glenda Fredman is a consultant clinical psychologist and systemic psychotherapist within the NHS. She contributes to a number of national public services and international organisations, where she works at all levels of organisations with service users in therapy, with staff in training, supervision and consultation, and with teams and organisations in consultation.

Working with Embodiment in Supervision

A systemic approach

Edited by Jo Bownas and Glenda Fredman

Routledge
Taylor & Francis Group
LONDON AND NEW YORK

First published 2017
by Routledge
2 Park Square, Milton Park, Abingdon, Oxon OX14 4RN

and by Routledge
605 Third Avenue, New York, NY 10017

Routledge is an imprint of the Taylor & Francis Group, an informa business

British Library Cataloguing in Publication Data
A catalogue record for this book is available from the British Library

Library of Congress Cataloging in Publication Data
Names: Bownas, Jo, 1956–editor. | Fredman, Glenda, 1955–editor.
Title: Working with embodiment in supervision: a systemic approach / edited by Jo Bownas and Glenda Fredman.
Description: Milton Park, Abingdon, Oxon; New York, NY: Routledge, 2016. | Includes index.
Identifiers: LCCN 2016001724 | ISBN 9781138024281 (hbk) | ISBN 9781138024298 (pbk) | ISBN 9781315762456 (ebk)
Subjects: LCSH: Psychotherapists—Supervision of. | Psychotherapy—Study and teaching—Supervision.
Classification: LCC RC459 .W66 2016 | DDC 616.89/14—dc23
LC record available at https://lccn.loc.gov/2016001724

ISBN: 978-1-138-02428-1 (hbk)
ISBN: 978-1-138-02429-8 (pbk)
ISBN: 978-1-315-76245-6 (ebk)

Typeset in Times New Roman
by Keystroke, Station Road, Codsall, Wolverhampton

Contents

Figures, exercises and guides

Figures

Exercises

Practice guides

Contributors

Taiwo Afuape is lead clinical psychologist and systemic psychotherapist at the Tavistock and Portman Foundation Trust, working in a Community CAMHS. She is lead systemic psychotherapist at Central and North West London Foundation Trust in Adult Mental Health. She regularly provides supervision, consultation and training to psychologists, therapists and other clinicians working in statutory and non-statutory agencies. She is author of *Power, Resistance and Liberation in Therapy with Survivors of Torture: To Have our Hearts Broken.*

Sharon Bond is a consultant systemic and family psychotherapist. She is Director of Chiron Consultation and Therapy Ltd and Chiron Training Ltd. She teaches and supervises systemic thinking and practice at The Institute of Family Therapy and Tavistock Clinic and at a North London Child and Adolescent Mental Health Service.

Jo Bownas is a consultant systemic and family psychotherapist and supervisor. She leads the family therapy service for West London Mental Health Trust, Forensic Service. She provides supervision and consultation to therapists and other practitioners working in the NHS, in social care, and in independent practice.

Catherine Butler is a lecturer on the Doctorate in Clinical Psychology at Bath University, where she also runs Foundation and Intermediate courses in systemic psychotherapy. She previously worked as a consultant clinical psychologist in the NHS, where she supervised clinical and counselling psychologists, IAPT workers, voluntary sector workers and students. She is co-editor of *Sex, Sexuality and Therapeutic Practice: A Manual for Therapists and Trainers.*

Glenda Fredman is a consultant clinical psychologist, systemic psychotherapist, trainer, and supervisor. She is director of training in systemic psychotherapy with Camden and Islington Mental Health Trust. She is author of *Death Talk: Conversations with Children and Families* and *Transforming Emotion: Conversations in Counselling and Psychotherapy*, and co-editor of *Being with Older People: A Systemic Approach.*

Olga Levitt practised for many years as an independent systemic psychotherapist, supervisor and trainer. Her supervision work focused on integrating the personal and professional life of supervisees. She teaches yoga with an emphasis on coping with the stresses of everyday life and runs workshops on yoga and mindfulness. Olga now teaches mindfulness with special training for therapists.

Philip Messent is a consultant family therapist working in CAMHS, in East London, for 30 years. He provides clinical and managerial supervision and consultation to practitioners working in statutory and non-statutory agencies. He contributes to training at the Institute of Family Therapy, and is active in developing international health links.

Nick Pendry is a social worker, systemic psychotherapist, trainer and supervisor. He is the Head of Clinical Practice and the Principal Child and Family Social Worker with the Royal Borough of Kensington and Chelsea. He works across the service directly with families, supervises practitioners and teaches at all levels of social work and systemic psychotherapy training.

Dr Janine Roberts is Professor Emerita, University of Massachusetts, Amherst, past president of AFTA (American Family Therapy Academy) and Associate Editor, International Scholarship, for *Family Process*. She has written *Tales and Transformations*; *Rituals for Our Times* (co-author); *Rituals in Families and Family Therapy* as well as 70 articles and chapters, and a poetry book, *The Body Alters*.

John Shotter is Emeritus Professor of Communication in the Department of Communication, University of New Hampshire, and a Research Associate, Centre for Philosophy of Natural & Social Science (CPNSS), London School of Economics, London. He is the author of *Social Accountability and Selfhood*; *Cultural Politics of Everyday Life: Social Constructionism, Rhetoric, and Knowing of the Third Kind*; *Conversational Realities: Constructing Life through Language*; *Conversational Realities Revisited: Life, Language, Body, and World*; and *Getting It: Witness-Thinking and the Dialogical . . . in Practice.*

Foreword

Openings

Dr Janine Roberts

This intriguing book is like ones we loved as children where you pulled a tab and a magical place appeared, numbers fanned open, or music sang out. Like those books, this one invites you to interact with its innovative, page-turning ideas in myriad ways – ways which will entice you and forever change your work. For example, Taiwo Afuape (chapter 7) takes you like a memoirist into her childhood as an elective mute in a proud and embodied Nigerian family, her later experiences with serious illness, and then links her story and work to profound ways to include the body in meaning making in supervision and therapy. At the end of her chapter, she artfully encourages you to focus on 'how you are leaving this chapter and how this chapter leaves you'. In chapter 9, about supervising therapeutic work involving intimate bodily experiences, Catherine Butler and Glenda Fredman ask you to reflect on your relationship to arousal and/or disgust by responding to two compelling vignettes, including one where a supervisee witnesses a small boy's toe fall off as a nurse is bathing him. When you begin chapter 10, Olga Levitt urges you to pause and think about what you 'sense in your body' as you delve into 'Mindfulness: Bringing body and breath to supervision'. She then offers you tantalising breathing and grounding exercises to help you be more aware of the interplay of your body, emotions, and thoughts. Nick Pendry and Philip Messent unpack their social identities in chapters 2 and 3 as a 'Black Indian man' and a 'White English male' with an open and deep integrity that provides terrific models about how to bring conversations about "race", power, privilege, and disempowerment into all levels of therapeutic work.

Working with Embodiment in Supervision: A Systemic Approach is groundbreaking and can be used across all theoretical orientations. It furrows new territory in more ways than I can elucidate in this short space, but let me tempt you with a few more examples. In chapter 4, 'Supervision as a cluster of conversations', Sharon Bond amplifies how we can enter into supervisory spaces by exploring 'how our emotions and bodily responses influence accountability' and demonstrates powerful techniques to make visible the invisible voices within clusters of conversations. She also works evocatively with why 'some conversations are bolder than others'. Jo Bownas (chapter 8) braids together ways we can be aware of our own 'lived-body' biographies as we trace body storylines, and then recognise bodily resonance between clients, supervisees and supervisors.

Her writing culminates with key ideas about how to develop a 'repertoire of possibilities' for body-focused supervision; ideas that are lucid, new to supervisory writing, and at the same time, eminently practical. Philip Messent skillfully takes us into zones of 'relational danger' in chapter 3, and shows how even in these spaces you can continue to stay open to new possibilities. He also delineates how ways we greet clients (and supervisees or supervisors for that matter) can strongly influence and shape therapeutic work. Furthermore, many of the ideas are organised into extremely useful templates like the Supervisor's Guide to 'Preparing ourselves for the therapeutic relationship', provided by Glenda Fredman in chapter 5, or the 'Guiding questions for mindful inquiry' (Olga Levitt, chapter 10).

What also makes the book absorbing is how each author grounds their writing in their journey to the ideas – a journey that often began because of what clients or supervisees asked, exposed, or taught them. For example, questions from eight-year-old Jill, whose mother had recently died, inspired Olga Levitt to break open her boundaries between yoga and therapy. As well, the contributors consistently write about when things did not go well and how they needed to be accountable and repair, or how they could do things differently in the future. Nick Pendry (chapter 2) explicates how he held back (as a Black Indian man supervising a White British woman who was working with a Black Nigerian family) from bringing "race" and racism into supervision, because he did not want her to 'think that I was identifying her or her practice as being racist'. Then he eloquently articulates four different ways he might have engaged with her about the "race" of the family, his "race", and hers, and power and privilege. You feel like you get to know each of the authors and who they are as learners, clinicians, and thinkers, at the same time as each chapter encourages you to expand how you know yourself in those arenas as a professional and personally.

Theory is also wonderfully explicated with richly described practice examples. This makes it very easy to transfer suggestions directly into your daily work while at the same time being aware of pitfalls because the authors so generously explain where they have stumbled. As well, this book has an unusual and helpful structure. At the end of each of the two parts, Jo Bownas and Glenda Fredman remark upon the chapters in that section and thread them together. This coheres the book in a way that is exceptional for an edited volume. Woven throughout is profound attention to how social difference and/or similarity is brought to our work via our bodies, accents, how we dress, and decorate our offices (or homes for those of us who do therapy and/or supervision there), or arrive at our clients' living spaces. It never feels tacked on like it can with books when authors superficially address multiculturalism, "race", ethnicity, class, gender, and sexual orientation.

The scope, depth, and variety of exercises, vignettes, and templates means you can use *Working with Embodiment in Supervision* for self-supervision, in group settings, or dyadic supervisor–supervisee relationships. Responding to questions in it and doing some of the activities helped me to process and think for example about how my bodily energies are different when I work with families (often more playful and relaxed), couples (more on alert), or individuals (sometimes more contemplative). I found myself with numerous strategies to more consciously locate myself in sessions as well as change emotional and body reactions.

As this book is written with such fluid openness, each person will find her or himself in new doorways and discovering unique paths. And if you do get lost, disoriented or just want company, you can always return to the eight wise guides and mentors who have created this vibrant book.

Dr Janine Roberts,
Longview House at Leverett Pond in
Western Massachusetts, August, 2015

Acknowledgements

There are many people who have contributed, knowingly or unknowingly, to the conception of this book and to its coming to fruition. Before we were supervisors we were supervisees, and we are immensely grateful to those supervisors who have shaped our practice and who continue to do so. For me, Jo, these include: Susan Lang, Adriana Penalosa Clarke, Grace Heaphy, Sanya Divac and John Burnham, with special appreciation to my individual supervisor, Glenda Fredman, and my peer supervision group, Margi Abeles and Maggie Smith, for the boundless curiosity, creativity and wisdom that have sustained me over many years. For me, Glenda, my early supervisors, Sylvia Duncan, Peter Reder, David Campbell and Adam Phillips profoundly shaped my practice as a therapist and continue to offer me a rich selection of role models to inform my supervisory practice. KCC and the wider systemic community offered rich and fertile soil for me to continue to grow and develop as a therapist and supervisor, as well as a safe place to return to refuel with courage to go on. Peter Lang's wisdom and generosity continue to nourish my vision of the sort of supervisor I would like to become; he has inspired me with the confidence to extend my abilities professionally and personally.

Friends of KCC continues to create a community in which ideas and ethical and innovative practice can flourish; this community supported the Embodiment in Supervision Conference (2013) that gave rise to this book. We thank especially Emily Strang, for her contribution to organising the conference, and all the presenters, whose workshops and plenaries inspired the book: Taiwo Afuape, Sharon Bond, John Burnham, Chris Hannah, Alfred Hurst, Olga Levitt, Adriana Penalosa Clarke, Nick Pendry, Gail Simon, Gerrilyn Smith, Yoko Totsuka and Anne Hedvig Vedeler.

All the authors of this book participated generously and with patience in the joint editing-writing process, making it possible for us, as editors, to engage personally with the material they offered. As the chapter drafts passed back and forth between us we were able to notice their effects on our bodies and their contributions to our developing supervision practice. Over time we have found ourselves further embodying the ideas and practices presented in the chapters, sometimes as a supervisor, a practitioner, supervisee or trainee. Their chapters have helped us as clinical supervisors 'stay present' and accompany our supervisees, colleagues and clients.

We are indebted to Elsa Jones and Janine Roberts for the inspiration they have given us as therapists, trainers and supervisors through their writings and trainings over many years and especially for their encouragement and support for this project. Eleanor Anderson and Philip Messent provided invaluable advice and suggestions on drafts of the book and Maggie Smith shared many helpful conversations along the way. We acknowledge with appreciation the contributions of Yoko Totsuka and Alfred Hurst, whose ideas (on power and difference and on self-disclosure) influenced our thinking and writing. Christine Landreth and Frances Landreth Strong's generous creativity produced the drawing for John Shotter's 'After words'.

We are very grateful to Joanne Forshaw, Kirsten Buchanan and Aiyana Curtis from Routledge for their helpful and responsive editorial assistance.

This book is full of stories of supervisors, supervisees and their clients, the ways they find of going on and the ideas and practices they develop together, which then become inspiration for others. We would like to acknowledge here, with deep gratitude, all the supervisees, trainees and clients whose willingness to share their stories and to explore new ground with us have shaped and inspired our practice.

1 Introduction

Bringing our bodies to supervision

Jo Bownas and Glenda Fredman

Introducing our selves

Since this book is about 'embodiment', we will begin by introducing our embodied selves to you, our reader. I (Jo Bownas) am a White[1] woman and my body has always been short in stature. My voice speaks to my English heritage and my vaguely middle-class social location. I (Glenda Fredman) am a White woman. I was born in Africa, in a Jewish family; throughout my childhood my Irish grandparents lived next door, and I was cared for tenderly by a Ndebele woman. I have also lived and worked for nearly 40 years in London. Our bodies show our advancing age in their contours, lines and tone. The ways in which we stand and sit, how we use our voice, hands and face, and how and what we receive and experience in our bodies are shaped by our life and work in our different cultures. These are the bodies with which we have read and responded to the contributions of the authors of this book and with which we write. Our bodies and the experiences and identities inscribed upon them have shaped our reading and writing; just as we anticipate that you, our reader, will be influenced in your reading of this book by your own embodiment.

Our bodies exist in social contexts and our professional contexts have also been present in the production of this book. I (Jo Bownas) am a systemic psychotherapist and supervisor, working in the public health service in a forensic mental health setting. I have also worked in child and adolescent mental health services and, earlier in my career, as a social worker in child and adult services. I (Glenda Fredman) am a clinical psychologist, systemic psychotherapist, supervisor and consultant. I have worked for over 30 years in the public health service, with people and their families facing trauma, illness and dying.

The stories we have heard, witnessed and lived through our personal and professional lives are written on our bodies, and they have been added to by the process of working on this book. Our eyes have become a little more strained, our typing hands a little stiffer, the lines on our faces a little deeper, our compassion heightened, our breathing sometimes slowed, sometimes accelerated, and we have also experienced a sense of movement and growth as we have become involved with the work of our author-colleagues. We have found ourselves embodying this growth in our professional contexts. We invite you, our reader, to bring your body to the reading of this book, to notice how your reading moves you and to consider how you might embody that movement within your own professional contexts.

How this book came about

The seeds of this book were planted during my (JB) supervision training between 2007 and 2009. As a trainee supervisor, teaching and supervising students in family therapy, I became aware of a gap in what I was offering my trainees. I had lots of ways of inviting trainees to reflect on and elaborate their use of language, but a limited repertoire of ways to explore and address how they were experiencing, thinking about and using their bodies when practising therapy. I noticed that we found it harder to talk in supervision about what we did with our bodies (tone of voice, posture, facial expression and gesture), expressions and activities that were often outside of our awareness while our minds were occupied with thinking about what we were saying. I also found myself asking how we could talk in our supervision groups about the embodied, felt experience of the therapist and team – the butterflies, headaches, racing pulse, sleepiness, heart sink, the feelings of anger or sadness, or the many other sensations we all experience in our work. How could we talk about these sensations and emotions in ways that were coherent with our systemic, social constructionist approach?

I remembered that when I began my own systemic therapy training we used to attend to digital and analogic, or verbal and non-verbal, communication (Watzlawick *et al.*, 1967). Although our focus at that time was more on the families' communication than on our own, we acknowledged that what our bodies do is part of communication. Therefore, in therapy sessions, we attended to how and where people sat and what they did with their bodies. Sometimes we invited people to move places or swap seats in the room (Minuchin and Minuchin, 1974). We also invited families to try out and comment on the effects of different bodily positions (Papp *et al.*, 1973; Papp *et al.*, 2013).

In supervision sessions with my supervisor, Glenda Fredman, we began to reflect on how attention to bodily experience and activity had waned as the systemic approach began to focus on what and how practitioners co-construct meaning *in language* with people in therapy (for example, Cecchin, 1992; Hoffman, 1992). Systemic therapists, like James Griffith and Melissa Elliot Griffith (1994) and Tom Andersen (1998), had brought the body back into focus in systemic therapy with clients and others, for example, Hoffman (1993) and Fredman (2004), had developed systemic approaches to working with emotion in therapy. But we noted an absence of attention to, and a dearth of literature on, bodily experience and activity in systemic and family therapy supervision. In particular, we recognised an absence of attention to, or use of, the body of the supervisor in the supervisory process.

I, therefore, went on to research 'embodiment in supervision' (Bownas, 2009) with a view to elaborating my repertoire of ways to think about, address and include bodily experiences, expression and activity in supervisory practice. For example, I invited experienced systemic therapy supervisors to a focus group to discuss how they thought about and worked with the body in supervision. Analysing their contributions using *Interpretive Phenomenological Analysis* (Smith *et al.*, 1999) and searching the literature revealed that there had been little attention to embodiment in supervision training or literature. Hence, supervisors like myself were drawing on the theories and practices of their preferred models of therapy, their encounters with ideas from beyond the world of therapy, and their own lived personal and professional experience to throw light on embodiment in supervision.

I, Glenda Fredman, was pleased to join Jo Bownas in exploring how we might bring our bodies into clinical supervision, by reflecting both *in* action and *on* the action of our own supervision practice (Schon, 1987). This exploration generated rich and creative practices for us both to use not only in our supervision sessions with each other but also in supervision with other supervisees (Bownas, chapter 8). We began wondering whether other colleagues were curious about or engaging with these sorts of processes and, together with Emily Strang, a family therapy colleague and co-organiser, we invited supervisors to share and reflect on experiences of 'embodiment in supervision' at a conference (Friends of KCC, 2013). The ideas and practices that emerged in the conference became the inspiration for this book.

In this book, we bring together a number of approaches to working with the body in clinical supervision. We offer a repertoire of practices for supervisors to reflect on, talk about and work with bodily experiences, expression and activity in supervisory practice. We address how, as practitioners and supervisors, we can use supervision to attend to what we feel, show and communicate with our bodies in practice. We also explore how we can use and make sense of our bodily feelings as well as perform with our bodies in clinical supervision. The chapters include examples of practice, exercises and practice guides which we hope will have immediate practical application for supervisors. However, it is not our intention as authors of this book to put forward a recipe for how things should be done. We present ideas and practices as offerings and invitations to you, our reader.

Our book is intended for supervisors of therapy, psychology and counselling approaches that are essentially language based, in which the body may more easily be overlooked. It should also be of interest to those who want to address embodiment in mental health. We expect that it would be a particularly useful text for trainers and trainees engaged in supervision training.

What is supervision?

The word 'supervision' is derived from the Latin '*super*' (over) and '*videre*' (to see), implying both a 'seeing' from a 'higher' vantage point and an 'overview' or 'watching over'. In this book, we approach supervision as encompassing both these understandings. We acknowledge that supervision has an 'overseeing', monitoring or evaluative purpose, with the intention of ensuring the welfare of clients and maintaining standards set by professional bodies and employing organisations; and we also see its purpose as to enrich the work with clients through a process in which practitioners reflect on their work, and their own development, facilitated by a (usually more experienced) supervisor, who offers a 'higher', or alternative perspective (Scaife, 2004). We are especially drawn to the work of supervisors practising within a narrative or social constructionist paradigm, who have questioned the hierarchical implications of the word 'supervision' and have offered alternatives that suggest a more collaborative relationship, such as 'share-vision' (Hoffman, 2001), 'co-vision' (White, 1997), 'collaborative conversation' (Anderson and Swim, 1995) or 'extra-vision' (Bird, 2006). However, we join these authors in cautioning against denying the supervisor's responsibility to 'review the counsellor's/therapist's practice according to ethical principles' (Bird, 2006: 112) or obscuring 'the power relation that is established by this privilege (of seniority, experience, rank)' (White, 1997: 148).

Contexts of supervision

The degree to which we emphasise hierarchy or egalitarianism, evaluation or reflection, direction or collaboration may be influenced by the context in which the supervision takes place (see Messent, chapter 3). The rights, duties and responsibilities of supervisee and supervisor may be different, or differently nuanced, for instance, depending on whether the supervision is privately contracted or is commissioned by the supervisee's employing agency; or whether the supervisee is a qualified practitioner or a trainee. In this book, we offer examples of supervision in different contexts, for instance, privately contracted supervision (Bownas, chapter 8; Levitt, chapter 10) and supervision in, or commissioned by, public services or statutory agencies, as well as independent organisations (Bond, chapter 4; Fredman, chapter 5; Afuape, chapter 7; Butler and Fredman, chapter 9). Philip Messent (chapter 3) addresses the additional complexity of supervision in which the supervisor holds responsibility for both managerial and clinical supervision within an agency. Nick Pendry (chapter 2) and Olga Levitt (chapter 10) include examples of supervision in a training context. All chapters offer exercises or practices that could be used in training, as well as in supervision of qualified practitioners.

Methods of supervision

Within these different contexts we, as supervisors, use different methods. Most chapters draw on experiences in individual supervision, in which supervisees bring stories of their work and dilemmas about the work for discussion with the supervisor. Chapters 3, 4 and 5 refer to peer or group supervision, in which a group of practitioners meets to reflect on their work, facilitated by a supervisor. Group members may be of the same or varied professions and may embody differences in, for instance, age, gender and ethnicity, bringing a multiplicity of perspectives to the supervision. Nick Pendry (chapter 2) and Philip Messent (chapter 3) give examples of live supervision in which the supervisor is present, either in the room or behind a one-way screen, during the therapy session. In systemic therapy the therapist often works with one or more 'team' colleagues; pre-session, mid-session and post-session team discussions create opportunities for supervision or peer supervision intended as reflexive practice. Taiwo Afuape (chapter 7) offers an example of videotape supervision in which the supervisee shows a recording of her work; introducing the possibility of reflection on how visible bodily identity and activity may be contributing to the work. Throughout the book, we also offer exercises that might be used in 'self-supervision', in which practitioners can use particular structures or frameworks to reflect on their selves and their own work.

Models of supervision

We acknowledge the rich development of models of supervision in the growing literature of supervision (for instance, Stoltenberg *et al.*, 1998; Wosket, 2001; Hawkins and Shohet, 2006; Madsen, 2014). In addition to drawing on models developed within the distinctive field of supervision, many supervisors also bring to their supervision practice the theoretical and methodological influence of their own therapeutic practice (Scaife, 2004). In this book, we offer supervision practices that draw on ways of understanding and acting that flow from our systemic, social constructionist and narrative approach to practice. In the following text, we will introduce you, our reader, to the principles guiding our approach to supervision. Systemic supervision clearly has a good fit for systemic therapists, but all the authors in this book also have experience of supervising practitioners of other disciplines – for example, doctors, social workers, psychologists, counsellors and practitioners of different models who have found systemic supervision helpful. We authors also draw on a range of influences within and beyond the field of systemic and family therapy, so we anticipate the book having a wide appeal to clinical supervisors working with a range of therapeutic models. Thus we hope that you, our reader, will find ideas and practices that are relevant to your supervision practice, whatever your profession or preferred guiding theories.

What is embodiment?

In this book we call attention to our bodies and to the bodies of our supervisees and their clients: what our bodies do, show, express and feel. It is in and with our physical, biological bodies that we feel and act in relation to ourselves, others and the environment. For us authors of this book, however, it is important that attention to our bodies does not return us to a focus on the objective and biologically-determined individual, skin-bounded self. Thus, we are drawn to Hardham's (1996: 75) use of the active word '**em**bodied' (emphasis is our own) rather than 'bodied', to indicate that 'embodiment' 'is not a quality that exists independently of relationships and connections'. 'Embodiment' describes not only how we experience and define our selves within the boundaries of our bodies, but also how 'we are boundaried, defined and located by others – and so we are also embodied by others' (Hardham, 1996: 75).

In this book, Taiwo Afuape (chapter 7) and Olga Levitt (chapter 10) question the body–mind dualism that has come to dominate 'Minority world' or 'Western' cultures. The French phenomenological philosophical movement rejected this Cartesian dualism, describing how 'the body is never simply a physical object but always an embodiment of consciousness' (Turner, 1996: 78). We are drawn to the work of John Shotter (2008: 29) who proposes a 'noncognitive, non-Cartesian, relationally-responsive, social constructionist approach to psychology as a *moral science*' in which we attend to *'the living body* . . . the spontaneously expressed, unreflective bodily activities of the whole person' since 'it is in sensuous bodily activities . . . that ideas start, not in "the mind"'. Turner (1996: 78) claims that discussion of the body leads us to a concern with intentions since, 'To perceive the world is to reflect upon possible actions of my body on the world.' Thus, we are interested in our bodies' actions and intention, but we are also concerned with how 'the world' acts upon our bodies. Thus, we embrace Hardham's (1996) proposal that, while we are 'embodied', we are also 'embedded' in social and relational contexts that give meaning to our bodies, actions and experiences. In this book, then, the word 'embodiment' encompasses what we feel in our bodies as physical sensations and emotions; what we do with our bodies, as in posture, gesture, tone of voice and what our bodies show of our identities, through visible differences such as "race",[2] "gender" or "age" or through how we choose to adorn our bodies.

Systemic supervision and embodiment

'Different kinds of supervision create different cultures and different cultures create different forms of supervision' (Burnham and Harris, 2002: 32). Therefore, we will introduce you, our reader, to some of the values, principles and commitments which we associate with systemic approaches, and to some of the systemic methods and techniques that both emerge from and reflexively re-create the 'culture' of systemic supervision (Burnham, 1992). These approaches, methods and techniques influence the theories we find attractive and affect how we prefer to see ourselves and to be known by others.

Attention to language and communication

Starting from the position that language is saying and doing, speaking and acting, throughout this book we pay careful attention to the language we use. Our belief that how we talk about people influences what they and we become, informs our approach to supervision and to our writing of the book. Therefore, we try to talk about the people with whom we work respectfully at all times, even when they are not with us, paying attention to not only the words or phrases we use but also how we communicate with our words and with our bodies. For example, recognising that our tone carries our intention, feeling and evaluative attitude (Shotter, 2006: 52), in chapter 5, Glenda Fredman addresses how to work with the pace, style and tone of supervisees' and supervisors' talk in supervision.

Including and reflecting on our selves in the process

All the authors in this book take a self-reflexive and relational–reflexive (Burnham, 2005) approach to supervision. That is, we situate ourselves in our personal and professional contexts, identify and question our own assumptions and consider the effects of our actions on our supervisees, on the client–therapist relationship and on the supervisor–supervisee relationship. Thus, in this book, we address supervision from different positions including those of supervisors, supervisees, clients and colleagues. We authors also take different personal positions in relationship to the material. Therefore, at times, we speak with our voices of family and culture or from positions of our gender, "race" or ethnicity in relation to our experience. At other times, we narrate with our professional voices in roles as supervisor, supervisee, trainer, trainee, therapist or consultant. We therefore move between references to 'clients', 'carers', 'professionals', 'practitioners', 'therapists', 'people', 'patients', 'families', 'colleagues' and 'participants' in an attempt to reflect the relationship that has emerged in the course of a particular episode of communication. You, our reader, may choose to take different positions during your reading of this book. For example, you may elect to read from the perspective of a supervisor, supervisee, trainer or client.

Competence and appreciation

In this book, we start from the premise that our meetings are more fruitful when people are involved in mutual listening, appreciation and respect, rather than defending, controlling, counter-justifying or blaming. Our position is informed and supported by our experiences with the clients and supervisees we meet, by systemic and narrative approaches and by outcome research demonstrating that effective therapists are those who are able to form a working alliance and have sophisticated facilitative interpersonal skills (Hubble *et al.*, 2010). The Milan systemic family therapy team (Selvini Palazzoli *et al.*, 1978) held the view that positively connoting people and their behaviour helps us appreciate the situation from each person's perspective; hence, we can more easily join with the client/supervisee and their system in working collaboratively towards their preferred outcomes. Boscolo *et al.* (1987) explained how it is harder for people to change under a negative connotation.

In chapter 5, Glenda Fredman attends to how telling and receiving negative, diminishing stories about the people with whom we are to meet can shape our bodies and influence the way we enter the encounter. She offers a pre-session supervision ritual to help us prepare our bodies so that we can meet people in 'emotional postures' (expressed in our bodies and our tone of voice) that invite mutual listening, appreciation and respect. Olga Levitt (chapter 10) describes how she uses mindfulness practice to prepare herself to meet her supervisees with non-judgemental acceptance and compassionate awareness. Drawing on the field of adult learning, for example the work of Belenky *et al.* (1997: 227) who describe how 'women found the experience of being doubted debilitating rather than energising', we aim to appreciate the competence and intentions of our supervisees. Therefore, we try to facilitate development by building on their strengths, abilities and resources (Todd and Storm, 2002). Butler and Fredman (chapter 9) describe how they work with supervisees who criticise and doubt their own abilities as practitioners when they have feelings of arousal or disgust arising with clients. They invite us as supervisors to consider our own responses when supervisees bring strong feelings to supervision that can draw us towards judging and interrogating the supervisee.

Impressed by the 'carefulness and genuine respect' of the Milan team, Tom Andersen (1987: 416) took the view that new ideas are more likely to invite new ways of relating if they are introduced within a relationship that is '"safe" enough, nonintrusive enough'. We believe that the stance of appreciation and respect showed by all the authors of this book contributes to the establishment of 'relational safety' (Mason, 2005; Hernández and Rankin, 2008) in supervision, as described by Philip Messent in chapter 3 and Nick Pendry in chapter 2. We also share the view that the relational culture of supervision creates patterns that are likely to be continued in the therapist–client relationship (Whiting, 2007), so that, in supervision, our chosen styles of relating act as offerings for our supervisees to carry into their own practice with clients.

Collaboration and power in supervision

Systemic approaches pay attention to differential power as it affects the lives of people with whom we meet and the relationships we can construct with them. Griffith and Elliot Griffith (1994: 73) note that hierarchies of power can silence people and, therefore, they 'strive to establish egalitarian relationships within the therapeutic conversation'. Anderson and Goolishian (1992) place their own knowledges and expertise alongside those of their clients and approach clients as experts on their own problems. In supervision Bobele *et al.* (1995: 17) address ways of viewing supervisory relationships that are 'not encumbered with some of the problems of hierarchy'. These approaches attend to the potential disqualifying practices of power and draw us towards collaborative relationships with supervisees. We may get into difficulty as supervisors, however, if we attempt entirely to erase the power differential inherent in our relationships with our supervisees since that erasure may paralyse us in fulfilling our responsibilities (Behan, 2003).

In this book, Nick Pendry (chapter 2) proposes that attempts to eradicate power relationships in supervision can allow supervisors to leave "race" and racism off the agenda. He gives an account of experiencing and resolving a dilemma about how he can fulfil his responsibility as the supervisor (to bring "race" into the conversation with a supervisee) without negatively connoting the supervisee or 'succumbing to the lure of authoritarianism' (Wilson, 1993: 177). Butler and Fredman (chapter 9) describe how they work with supervisees who criticise and doubt their own abilities as practitioners when they have feelings of arousal and disgust. Bond (chapter 4) introduces us to 'Domains of Action' in which the supervisor may choose explicitly to work *with* her supervisee for a time in the evaluative, action-orientated 'domain of production'. Messent (chapter 3) gives an account of his experience as a manager, charged with ensuring his supervisees work to the standards and priorities of the agency. He describes the difficulties that can arise in this role and the practices he engages in to maintain collaborative and generative relationships, while acknowledging the power of his position and its intersection with the privilege associated with his identity as a White man.

Inviting multiple perspectives and not knowing too quickly

The use of questions, rather than statements, interpretations or suggestions is central to the systemic method (Tomm, 1988). In particular, we use relational questions to invite the people with whom we are meeting to consider connections and differences between people and ideas, between our actions and the meanings we give to those actions and the contexts in which we act. In supervision we intend that our supervisees, in listening to our questions and their own answers, will make new connections and that our questions will keep us, as supervisors, open to multiple views of the situation (Todd, 2002: 191). Our preference for questions (to which there is no assumption of 'right' answers) is also intended to restrain our own 'knowing' too soon, since becoming absorbed in our own knowledge can disconnect us from our supervisees and lead us to offer ideas or 'solutions' that are not useful because they are not sufficiently close to the supervisee's concern or do not invite new thinking. We do not disregard our knowledge or ideas but we think of them as 'hypotheses' that guide our questions while we remain 'curious' (Cecchin, 1987) to know *from* our supervisees. Burnham and Harris (2002) describe a practice of 'withholding, with-holding' in which the supervisor holds back on immediately sharing his or her own ideas, instead 'holding' the supervisee/s while they discuss their own ideas, generating self-reflexive learning.

All the authors in this book show their preference for this stance of questioning, curiosity and for *not knowing too quickly*. For example, they appreciate that our bodies and their expressions and responses can be held as private and drawing attention to them in supervision could be experienced as intrusive. Therefore, Levitt (chapter 10) and Bownas (chapter 8) ask their supervisees' consent to engage in '*body talk*', or '*body practice*' and Butler and Fredman (chapter 9) start with '*talking about talking*', to explore whether the supervisee wishes to engage in a conversation about their bodily experience. Afuape (chapter 7) offers questions that explore the cultural contexts of her supervisee's preferences for bodily closeness and distance. In videotape supervision, she shows how she uses questions (rather than comments or observations) to invite her supervisee's reflection on his use of his body. Bond (chapter 4) shows how she uses questions to invite the emergence of her supervisee's preferred identities and to explore how the supervisee's bodily feelings may point to dissonances with her preferred identities, preventing her from 'giving an account' of her work that would enable her to go on. Levitt offers the practice of *Mindful Enquiry*, in which she uses questions to invite her supervisee to attend to the experience of her body during mindfulness practice and to notice connections she makes with her work.

Many of the authors of this book use versions of *reflecting teams* (Andersen, 1987; Lax, 1995; Roberts, 2002) to present and value multiple perspectives. The supervisor or another supervisee interviews the therapist/supervisee who may be one or more practitioners. The other supervisees listen to the interview while they talk. At a time agreed with those being interviewed, the listening supervisees talk about what they have heard while the interviewer and those who were interviewed listen. This creates an opportunity for those 'reflecting' to offer multiple perspectives for supervisees to hear different conversations (see Bond, chapter 4, and Fredman, chapter 5, for examples).

Reading and writing this book

The authors of this book offer personal stories, transcripts of conversations and case vignettes, wherever possible to 'speak' the theory and demonstrate the practices they describe. In order to ensure that the people presented cannot be recognised by others, we have changed names and other potentially identifying characteristics. In some situations, we have merged examples or combined the experiences or reports of different people to construct one composite 'profile'. This approach is intended to protect anonymity further.

The book is divided into two parts to point you, our reader, towards the emphasis of the different sections. 'Part I: Power and difference embodied in the supervision process' starts from the position that our personal and professional identities, including aspects of social difference and differential power and privilege, are written on our bodies through, for example, the colour of our skin, the male/femaleness of our shape, the smoothness or the lines of our faces. The authors discuss how the *meanings* of our bodies are not biologically determined, but are socially constructed in interaction with others and embedded in social contexts. Thus, while the colour of our skin, our sex and the development and decline of our bodies may be part of our physiology, the concepts of "race", "gender" and "age" are social constructs; and these social constructs are associated with differential power and privilege. The chapters in Part I, therefore, address the implications for supervision practice of this embodiment of identity and difference and include chapters on issues of minority exclusion and discrimination, written by those who have experienced marginalisation as well as members of the dominant group.

'Part II: Using our bodies with intention in supervision', starts from the position that we meet each other with our bodies in clinical practice and supervision, speaking with our words and also with our bodies – with bodily position, posture and gesture; with tone of voice; with our felt bodily responses to each other (Shotter, 2008). The chapters address how, as practitioners, we engage and communicate through and with our bodies and how our bodies express and are affected by our experience of the work we do. The authors introduce us to the varied practices they have evolved for working with physical sensation, emotion and bodily movements in supervision. They attend to how felt bodily experience may contribute to meaning making in supervision and how, in turn, we may use our bodies' movements to influence us in preferred directions in our work. The authors offer supervisory practices to guide practitioners to attend to and use their bodies with intention to facilitate therapeutic relationships.

There is no hard line distinguishing the two parts of the book, which is coherent with our approach to supervision in which we seldom seek hard lines, but are interested in the fluid and co-evolutionary development of practice that draws on many sources for its inspiration. Therefore, rather than compartmentalise, all the authors have woven attention to contexts of power and privilege throughout the practice they share in this book.

We, the authors of this book, address some of the questions and dilemmas encountered by clinical supervisors in relation to the embodied selves of therapist, client and supervisor and draw attention to these questions in a field where a focus on language may have left us 'disembodied'. Whilst there has been some interest in the theme of embodiment in therapy literature, we, like Hardham (1996), make a distinction between an understanding of the therapist's 'use of self' which emphasises language and narrative and one which includes attention to the unintentional (pre-reflective) and intentional expressions and constructions of the physical body. It is this latter understanding, less frequently addressed in the supervision literature, that will be the distinctive focus of this book.

We, the editors, have read and re-read these chapters checking and corresponding with our author colleagues about the meanings of words for them, what they wanted phrases to 'do' for the reader and how this was important to them. In our reading, as we have allowed their words to touch us and move us to different positions, we noticed how we began to embody the writing in our work and our lives. We also became fascinated with how our experiences, felt responses and learning from what we read were affected by whom we were embodying as we were reading the chapters. For example, we saw, felt and made sense differently when we read through eyes and positions of our clients, supervisees, teachers, managers or critics, through the eyes and bodies (including voices) of our authors and through the embodiment of each other. As Sharon Bond shows in chapter 4, the diversity of this cluster of conversations can offer us a richness from which to draw and create, as well as the discomfort and inspiration that comes of the 'tension' involved in the process of collaborative creativity.

We are grateful to our author-colleagues for working so graciously with us on this project. Mindful that writing is personal and that our author-colleagues have been bringing their selves and their bodies to the page, we want to honour and give back something of how we have been moved, touched and affected by what the chapters have offered us. Therefore, in chapters 6 and 11, we aim to continue the conversations by reflecting on how we have embodied the chapters offered by our author-colleagues. To facilitate this process, we have adapted Michael White's (2007) 'outsider witnessing practices' which he developed to help practitioners stay tuned to people's stories, unique knowledges and skills by centring the client and decentring themselves. Michael White invited witnesses to reflect on how they had been touched and moved by what the clients told and then to speak of what resonated for them, what they learned from the clients' experience and where this might take them. You, our reader, might like to use our version of these questions (Exercise 1.1) after your reading of the chapters to explore your embodiment of the writings and reflect on where they have taken you.

Exercise 1.1 Questions to explore our embodiment of the chapters in this book

- What struck you?
  What were you drawn to?
  What stood out for you/caught your attention?
- What images did the reading bring to mind?
  How does this connect with what is important to you? Why is this important for you?
- What connections do you make with your own supervision/practice?
  What resonates with your personal or professional experiences in your own life/work?
  What examples or stories does this bring to mind?
- Where has this taken you?
  What have you learned from the chapter/s?
  What new ideas have emerged?
  How might you use this in the future?
  What will you take forward in your practice/supervision?

(Adapted from White, 2007)

Notes

1 Guided by the writing conventions of the American Psychological Association (2010), we capitalise White and Black as proper nouns that 'represent the human beings we are referring to when using these terms' (Pewewardy and Almeida, 2014: 231) except when the terms are not capitalised in direct quotations. We do not capitalise when 'white' and 'black' are used to denote or qualify processes or common nouns e.g. white privilege, whiteness, black perspectives.

2 Our use of inverted commas with "race", "age" and "gender" denotes our reference to the social construction of these concepts in the context in which we are referring to them. See also Nick Pendry (chapter 2) for further discussion of the social construction of "race".

References

American Psychological Association (2010) *Publication Manual of the American Psychological Association (6th Ed.).* Washington DC: Author.

Andersen, T. (1987) The reflecting team: dialogue and metadialogue in clinical work. *Family Process*, 26, 415–28.
Andersen, T. (1998) One sentence of five lines about creating meaning. *Human Systems: The Journal of Systemic Consultation and Management*, 9, 73–80.
Anderson, H. and Goolishian, H. (1992) The client is the expert: a not-knowing approach to therapy. In S. McNamee and K. Gergen (eds). *Therapy as Social Construction.* Newbury Park, CA: Sage.
Anderson, H. and Swim, S. (1995) Supervision as collaborative conversation: connecting the voices of supervisor and supervisee. *Journal of Systemic Therapies*, 14, 1–13.
Behan, C. P. (2003) Some ground to stand on: narrative supervision. *Journal of Systemic Therapies*, 22(4), 29–41.
Belenky, M. F., Clinchy, B. M., Goldberger, N. R. and Tarule, J. M. (1997) *Women's Ways of Knowing.* New York: Basic Books.
Bird, J. (2006) *Constructing the Narrative in Supervision.* Auckland: Edge Press.
Bobele, M., Gardner, G. T. and Biever, J. L. (1995) Supervision as social construction. *Journal of Systemic Therapies,* 14(2), 14–25.
Boscolo, L., Cecchin, G., Hoffman, L. and Penn, P. (1987) *Milan Systemic Family Therapy.* New York: Basic Books.
Bownas, J. (2009) Working with the embodied self in systemic supervision and training. *Masters in Systemic Practice (Supervision and Training), Unpublished MA dissertation.* KCC & University of Bedfordshire.
Burnham, J. (1992) Approach-method-technique: making distinctions and creating connections. *Human Systems: The Journal of Systemic Consultation and Management*, 3(1), 3–26.
Burnham, J. (2005) Relational reflexivity: a tool for socially constructing relationships. In C. Flaskas, B. Mason and A. Perlesz (eds). *The Space Between: Experience, Context and Process in the Therapeutic Relationship.* London: Karnac.
Burnham, J. and Harris, Q. (2002) Cultural issues in supervision. In D. Campbell and B. Mason (eds). *Perspectives in Supervision.* London: Karnac.
Cecchin, G. (1987) Hypothesising, circularity and neutrality revisited: an invitation to curiosity. *Family Process*, 26, 405–13.
Cecchin, G. (1992) Constructing therapeutic possibilities. In S. McNamee and K. J. Gergen (eds). *Therapy as Social Construction.* London: Sage.
Fredman, G. (2004) *Transforming Emotion: Conversations in Counselling and Psychotherapy.* London: Whurr.
Friends of KCC Conference (2013) *Embodiment in Supervision.* Conway Hall, London.
Griffith, J. L. and Elliott Griffith, M. (1994) *The Body Speaks: Therapeutic Dialogues for Mind-Body Problems.* New York: Basic Books.
Hardham, V. (1996) Embedded and embodied in the therapeutic relationship: understanding the therapist's use of self systemically. In C. Flaskas. and A. Perlesz (eds). *The Therapeutic Relationship in Systemic Therapy.* London: Karnac.
Hawkins, P. and Shohet, R. (2006) *Supervision in the Helping Professions.* Maidenhead and New York: Open University Press.
Hernández, P. and Rankin, P. (2008) Relational safety in supervision. *Journal of Marital and Family Therapy*, 34, 58–74.
Hoffman, L. (1992) A reflexive stance for family therapy. In S. McNamee and K. J. Gergen (eds). *Therapy as Social Construction.* London: Sage.
Hoffman, L. (1993) *Exchanging Voices: A Collaborative Approach to Family Therapy.* London: Karnac Books.

Hoffman, L. (2001) *Family Therapy: An Intimate History.* New York: W.W. Norton.
Hubble, M. A., Duncan, B. L., Miller, S. D. and Wampold, B. E. (2010) Introduction. In B. L. Duncan, S. D. Miller, M. A. Hubble and B. E. Wampold (eds). *The Heart and Soul of Change: Delivering What Works* (2nd Ed.). Washington DC: American Psychological Association.
Lax, W. D. (1995) Offering reflections: some theoretical and practical considerations. In S. Friedman (ed.). *The Reflecting Team in Action: Collaborative Practice in Family Therapy.* New York: Guilford Press.
Madsen, W. C. (2014) Applications of collaborative helping maps: supporting professional development, supervision and work teams in family centred Practice. *Family Process*, 53(1), 3–21.
Mason, B. (2005) Relational risk-taking and the training of supervisors. *Journal of Family Therapy,* 27, 298–301.
Minuchin, S. and Minuchin, P. (1974) *Families and Family Therapy.* Cambridge, MA: Harvard University Press.
Papp, P., Silverstein, O. and Carter, E. (1973) Family sculpting in preventive work with well families. *Family Process*, 12, 197–212.
Papp, P., Scheinkman, M. and Malpas, M. (2013) Breaking the mold: sculpting impasses in couples' therapy. *Family Process*, 52(1), 33–45.
Pewewardy, N. and Almeida, R. V. (2014) Articulating the scaffolding of white supremacy: the act of naming in liberation. *Journal of Progressive Human Services*, 25, 230–53.
Roberts, J. (2002) Reflecting processes and'supervision': looking at ourselves as we work with others. In T. C. Todd and C. L. Storm (eds). *The Complete Systemic Supervisor.* Lincoln, NE: Authors Choice Press.
Scaife, J. (2004) *Supervision in the Mental Health Professions.* Hove and New York: Brunner–Routledge.
Schon, D. A. (1987) *Educating the Reflective Practitioner.* San Francisco: Jossey-Bass Publishers.
Selvini Palazzoli, M., Boscolo, L., Cecchin, G. and Prata, G. (1978). *Paradox and Counterparadox.* New York: Aranson.
Shotter, J. (2006) Vygotsky, Bakhtin, Goethe: consciousness and the dynamics of voice. Paper given in the Department of Communication, University of California at San Diego, May 3rd, 2006.
Shotter, J. (2008) *Conversational Realities Revisited: Life, Language, Body and World.* Chagrin Falls, Ohio: Taos Institute Publications.
Smith, J. A., Jarman, M. and Osborn, M. (1999) Doing interpretative phenomenological analysis. In M. Murray and K. Chamberlain, K. (eds). *Qualitative Health Psychology: Theories and Methods*. London: Sage.
Stoltenberg, C. D., McNeill, B. and Delworth, U. (1998) *IDM Supervision: An Integrated Developmental Model for Supervising Counsellors and Therapists.* San Francisco: Jossey-Bass.
Todd, T. C. (2002) Purposive systemic supervision models. In T. C. Todd and C. L. Storm (eds). *The Complete Systemic Supervisor.* Lincoln, NE: Authors Choice Press.
Todd, T. C. and Storm, C. L. (2002) *The Complete Systemic Supervisor.* Lincoln, NE: Authors Choice Press.
Tomm, K. (1988) Interventive Interviewing. Part III: intending to ask lineal, circular, strategic or reflexive questions. *Family Process*, 27, 1–15.
Turner, B. S. (1996) *The Body and Society.* London: Sage.

Watzlawick, P., Beavin, J. and Jackson, D. D. (1967) *Pragmatics of Human Communication: A Study of Interactional Patterns Pathologies and Paradoxes.* New York: W.W. Norton.

White, M. (1997) *Narratives of Therapists' Lives.* Adelaide, South Australia: Dulwich Centre Publications.

Whiting, J. B. (2007) Authors, artists, and social constructionism: a case study of narrative supervision. *The American Journal of Family Therapy*, 35, 139–50.

Wilson, J. (1993) The supervisory relationship in family therapy training: constructing a fit between trainee and trainer. *Human Systems: The Journal of Systemic Consultation and Management*, 4, 173–88.

Wosket, V. (2001) The cyclical model of supervision: a container for creativity and chaos. In M. Carroll and M. Tholstrup (eds). *Integrative Approaches to Supervision.* London and Philadelphia: Jessica Kingsley.

Part I

Power and difference embodied in the supervision process

2 The construction of racial identity

Implications for clinical supervision

Nick Pendry

> Race doesn't really exist for you because it has never been a barrier. Black folks don't have that choice.[1]
>
> (Chimamanda Ngozi Adichie, *Americanah*, 2013: 46)

I am a Black Indian man who was adopted by White British parents as an infant. I grew up, was educated and now live and work in a White-dominated British society. In my professional life I am a social worker, a systemic psychotherapist and supervisor, working in a local government children's services department in London. For me, "race" has always existed, in the way that I think about myself, my relationships, where I can go out to eat and drink, where I holiday, where I live. For those with whom I come to be in relationship, in whatever context, my "race" constructs for them ideas about who I am, and what characteristics I might have, which profoundly influences the way in which they relate to me. "Race" is an inescapable reality.

In this chapter, I aim to articulate what I mean by this reality of "race" in the field of therapy and supervision, in large part from my experiences as a practitioner and supervisor of clinical practice in a British context. In this British social and political context, as in most of what might be termed the Western world, the idea of "race" is as significant as ever. I take the position that "race" is a major organising principle in everyday life (Hardy, 2008), and that the social reality of racism has a huge influence in the lives and relationships of us all (Pendry, 2012). Skin colour is usually at the centre of constructions of "race". Increasingly religion, culture and language, as well as what we choose to wear or how we adorn our bodies to express our cultures and religions, are seen as indicators of racial difference, although these indicators are most often confirmed by a difference in skin tone. In this way our bodies point to our "race", and this fact is then used by others to form ideas about who we are, what political affiliation we might hold, the religion we might practise and the way in which we might relate to family and friends.

In the theory and practice of psychotherapy the idea of "race", and the reality of racism have received increasing, although still limited, attention in relation to practice and supervision. I see this relative lack of attention to "race" and racism as a political issue. By virtue of the power they hold, in relation to individual clients and families, clinicians can practise in a way that perpetuates or challenges inequality, such as the inequality between White and Black people. Similarly, supervisors in their positions of power, in relation to supervisees, can supervise in the interests of promoting racial equality, rather than, through inattention to this, inadvertently reinforcing the inequitable status quo. I take the position that clinical supervisors need to challenge inequality to enable ethical and useful working relationships; and that they hold the responsibility for drawing attention to embodied social difference and initiating conversations about "race" and racism.

Talking about "race" and racism with clients or supervisees may involve a level of anxiety and fear given the emotive subject matter. I will, therefore, discuss how the supervisor can establish a supervisory context that opens space for taking relational risks (Mason, 2005), to explore how "race" might be influencing relationships between themselves and supervisees, and between the supervisee and their clients. I offer self-reflexive exercises that I use to facilitate these sorts of conversations. I will offer a practice framework for talking about "race" and addressing racism within clinical supervision for the supervisor to introduce as an ongoing part of the supervision relationship.

I will begin by addressing the construction of "race", before considering how "race" and racism have been addressed within the field of therapy and the supervision of clinical practice. While I draw on examples from my practice, as a family and systemic psychotherapist, the ideas and practices I have developed have wider applicability across the psychotherapy field.

The construction of "race"

The use of "race" as a construct with which to categorise people emerged in a European context in the nineteenth century, with the acceptance of two key beliefs: firstly, that there are intrinsic psychological differences between the different "races" and secondly, that only people of one "blood", can share the same cultural and intellectual heritage (Miller *et al.*, 1987). The seemingly biological foundation of this categorisation of people into "races" with different genetic characteristics, including intelligence, persisted into the twentieth century, and can be seen to remain influential in politics, the media, and the education system. In the United Kingdom, for instance, this can be seen in the political commentary about the apparent failing educational achievements of young Black boys (REACH report, 2007; Equality and Human Rights Commission, 2010) and in the media debate about whether Black sportsmen can be seen to be ethnically British (BBC, *Newsbeat*, 30.09.09).

In the late twentieth and into the twenty-first century, an understanding of "race" as a social construct has gained ascendancy, although the influence of a pseudo-biological discourse of "race" remains in evidence. In genetic terms the biological differences between groups defined as "races" have been shown to be trivial, leaving the idea of "race" without empirical substance (Dalal, 2002). Smedley and Smedley (2005) outline that the consensus among most scholars in fields, such as evolutionary biology, anthropology and other disciplines, is that racial distinctions fail on all three counts; that is, they are not genetically discrete, are not reliably measured, and are not scientifically meaningful. Thus, all that remains is a social construction, which leads people and institutions to *act as if* the idea of "race" is a fixed objective category (Solomos, 2003). "Race", then, is best understood as a political and social construct; that is, an organising discursive category around which has been established a system of socio-economic power, exploitation and exclusion (Gunaratnam, 2003).

Physical appearance in terms of skin colour, in particular, is largely the foundation upon which this construction of "race" is based (Renn, 2012), with an apparently popular shared understanding. This can be seen in the use of the reductionist terms 'black' and 'white' to classify people into racial groupings. It is this reductionist process that has given rise to the political understanding of the term 'black' as referring to those who share similar experiences of oppression as a result of belonging to visible ethnic minority groups (Dalal, 2002).

The ideologies and actions that discriminate against others on the basis of their putatively different racial membership is the process of racism (Solomos, 2003). The idea of "race" leads to the different treatment of people according to differences in skin colour, with Black people mostly suffering the negative consequences of racism. This marks a distinct paradox in that, despite evidence that "race" is not a biological reality, the *social meanings* given to embodied difference, to "racial" categories and the people who belong to them, are as powerful as ever (Renn, 2012). At both individual and collective levels, "race" and its product, racism, matter. The different treatment of people on the basis of their "race" is produced and reproduced through political discourse, the media and the education system, serving to perpetuate racist understandings of particular social issues (Pendry, 2012). In the case of street crime in the United Kingdom, for instance, it has long been acknowledged that more young Black men are stopped and searched by the police, on suspicion of criminal activity, than any other racial grouping (Ministry of Justice, 2008; Equality and Human Rights Commission, 2013), serving the racist belief that Black men are more likely to be involved in criminal activity as a direct result of their skin colour.

"Race", racism and clinical practice

In understanding racism as a system of advantage, which involves discriminatory institutional policies and practices together with the discriminatory actions of individuals (Tatum, 1997), the field of psychological therapy can be seen as a further site for the perpetuation of racism. This field has, for example, been involved in the disproportionate diagnosis of young Black men with serious mental health difficulties, leading to their higher admission rates to psychiatric hospitals in the United Kingdom (Count Me In, 2010), and has conceptualised the family as an intact, middle-class, heterosexual, white unit, with the man located as the head of the household and the woman as the primary caretaker of family relationships (McGoldrick and Hardy, 2008).

The influence of multiple levels of oppression upon lives and relationships is often not taken into account in clinical practice when considering explanations for mental health or family problems. Ignoring the relevance of oppression and unearned privilege in clinical practice risks leaving societal systems of domination unchallenged. In the systemic psychotherapy field the influence of unequal gender relations in the difficulties presented in therapy began to be recognised in the writings particularly of Hare-Mustin (1978), James and McIntyre (1983) and Goldner (1988), although the influence of the idea of "race" has remained largely hidden until relatively recently. The writings of Boyd-Franklin (1989), McGoldrick (1998), Hardy and Laszloffy (2000) and Erskine (2002) began to address the way in which the impact of "race" and racism might be thought about in a therapeutic context, although this is still a marginalised area. As Singh (2009: 378) comments, in clinical terms in large part, '"the family" is still defined in Eurocentric terms by clinicians who are predominantly American and European'.

The fields of therapy and counselling need to take account of the idea of "race" as a major organising principle in everyday life. The reality of racism cannot be ignored, for this leaves every White person with access to white privilege, with its unearned benefits of options, opinions and opportunities, whilst leaving Black people disproportionately and intractably overrepresented in targeted groups of inequity (Hardy, 2008; Almeida *et al.*, 2011). In order for these fields to shift towards challenging a pro-racist ideology in clinical practice, we need to talk about "race" and the process of racism. This can be difficult given the emotionally charged nature of the subject, the history of unequal race relationships including the legacy of slavery and colonialism, and the tendency in a cross-racial context to retreat into polarised positions (Erskine, 2002; Hardy, 2008). However, I take the position that, both collectively and individually, all therapists have a moral and ethical duty to challenge the inequality of racism.

Creating a context for addressing "race" and racism: exercises in self-reflexivity

We can begin to talk about "race" and racism within a clinical supervision context, by inviting supervisees in individual or group supervision, or as a private exercise, to take the time to reflect upon their own racial identity and the influence that they think this might have on the supervisory relationship and their work with client families.

Reflecting on our racial identities in supervision

Drawing upon the work of Hardy (2008), I have used the following questions (Exercise 2.1) in various supervision and training contexts to engage clinicians in this process. Each time I use these questions I am struck by the way in which the simple asking of them can lead to the generation of new information for clinicians about how they locate themselves in relation to "race" and racism. I invite you, the reader, to take some time to consider these questions for yourself.

Exercise 2.1 Reflecting on our racial identities in supervision

- How do I define myself racially?
- What meaning(s) do I attach to who I am racially?
- What ideas and beliefs do I have that are informed by "race"?
- How does "race" inform my intimate relationships?
- How does my "race" facilitate interactions with members of another "race"?
- How is my "race" a detriment or obstacle to my interactions with members of another "race"?

Within supervision, I invite supervisees to consider how their responses to these questions might directly be influencing their practice. When we, as supervisors, address the influence of our own racial identity on our practice with supervisees in a reciprocal process throughout the supervisory relationship, we are able to model to the practitioner how to work with clients in a parallel process.

Using literature and film to raise consciousness of the influence of "race" and racism

I have also invited supervisees to view a particular film or read a particular novel to raise consciousness of the influence of "race" in their professional relationships and clinical practice, and to introduce social context and social location as departure points for later conversations (Hernández and McDowell, 2010). For example, I use a video clip of the Black Jamaican British writer and poet, Benjamin Zephaniah, performing a poem and discussing the issue of "race" and racism from a very personal perspective (Zephaniah, 2012). After viewing this video clip I ask supervisees to consider the following questions.

Exercise 2.2 Using literature and film to raise consciousness of the influence of "race" and racism

- What was your personal response while watching this clip? How did you feel?
- How do you think your response was influenced by your own racial identity and the positions of oppression and/or of privilege that your racial identity affords you?

The evocative material and the questions have brought forth moving personal accounts from my supervisees, and opened space for them to specifically consider how histories of oppression and legacies of privilege might be at work in their own personal and professional lives and relationships.

Once supervisors have facilitated an enabling relational context for conversations about racial identity, privilege and oppression in this way, they need to continually engage their supervisees in this self-reflexive process. Later in this chapter I will offer further exercises that can contribute to keeping the conversation alive.

Bringing "race" and racism to supervision: whose job is it?

The literature addressing the idea of "race" and the process of racism within supervision offers a clear challenge to supervisory practice with the message that "race" and racism should be a part of the discourse in supervision at both the level of the supervisory relationship and of the relationship between supervisee and clients (Arnold, 1993; Lawless *et al.*, 2001). Ayo's (2010: 236) small qualitative research project shows that both supervisors and supervisees share the idea that "race" and racism should be part of the discourse in supervision. The supervisors participating in her study accepted responsibility for initiating and maintaining talk of "race". The supervisees thought that it was important that supervisors take responsibility to raise these issues, but that it was a shared responsibility.

Hernández and McDowell (2010) assert that supervision informed by a postcolonial perspective, a form of supervision that challenges existing inequalities and the structures that maintain these inequalities, requires supervisors and supervisees to acknowledge histories of oppression and be accountable for the legacies of privilege within their local and global contexts. If, as in my supervisory practice with Ruth below, embodied social difference is ignored and "race" and racism is left off the supervisory agenda, we risk maintaining rather than challenging racial inequality.

> I, an experienced, male family therapist of Black Indian ethnicity, was live-supervising Ruth, a female family therapy trainee of White British ethnicity. Ruth was working with a family of Black Nigerian ethnicity, consisting of a mother, father and their son (eight years old) and daughter (11 years old). The son was referred to the Children and Young People's Service, in which we work, due to a pattern of violent and verbally abusive behaviour, particularly directed towards adult women at school and at home. In the pre-session discussion, before Ruth's fifth meeting with the family, she talked about feeling 'unable to work with this family to make change', and expressed the view that she thought there was 'no hope' for this family. I engaged Ruth in a conversation in which we thought together about what losing hope for this family might mean for her as a practitioner and how this might be influencing her work with the family. My primary hypothesis was concerned with Ruth's relative lack of experience in working with family members together in a systemic way, since she tended to take a therapeutic position in the work of imploring

> the son to change his violent and abusive behaviour. I suggested this possibility to Ruth by inviting her to consider how this lack of experience, in working with multiple family members, might be organising her to focus particularly upon the son's behaviour as an individual problem to be solved. Ruth responded to this invitation by stating that she was going to be 'more systemic' in her approach and only ask relational questions in the following session; she appeared relieved to have an understanding of what was happening in her work with this family.

I had not invited Ruth to address the "race" of this boy and his family. Neither she nor I raised the possibility that the construction of this family's "race" might be influencing her idea about the family's ability to change. Not talking about "race" and racism risks all supervisees receiving the message that these issues are unimportant and risks Black supervisees of White supervisors experiencing direct racism within the supervisory relationship (Cook, 1994). In turn supervisees will have less awareness of the organising impact of "race" and racism upon the lives of their clients, and indeed themselves, and so be lacking in their capacity to assess, plan and provide appropriate treatment (Hernández *et al.*, 2009). In this way, we risk perpetuating racism and poor practice. I will return to this example later in the chapter, exploring how we might move from not talking to talking about "race" and racism.

Practical steps towards challenging a pro-racist ideology in supervision

The question of how conversations about "race" and racism might begin to form an integral part of the supervisory relationship has been addressed in various ways. Divac and Heaphy (2005) have proposed the 'Space for GRRAACCES', whereby a designated space, wholly focused on facilitating the development of cultural competence, is created within a formal supervision and training programme. In this environment trainees and supervisees explore their culturally determined beliefs, values and attitudes through various personal exercises (for example, Totsuko, 2014) intended to develop their sense of their own culture and ethnicity and attention to which voices become dominant and privileged or silenced and subjugated (Divac and Heaphy, 2005).

Tracking the impact of "race" on our personal and professional lives

In my supervision practice I invite supervisees to track their personal and professional paths into their current position, focusing particularly upon how they think their own racial identity has promoted or constrained them. This has the effect of supporting the supervisees to consider the organising impact of "race" upon their lives in often previously unconsidered ways. In this exercise, I interview supervisees using the following questions as a guiding framework.

Exercise 2.3 Tracking the impact of "race" on our personal and professional lives

- How did you come to be in your current employment/training position?
  - What important (personal/professional) steps do you identify in your journey to where you are now?
- How do you think your experiences of "race" and racism and your racial identity have influenced your personal and professional development and vice-versa?
  - How might your racial identity and experience have supported/hindered you occupying your preferred personal and professional positions?

I use these questions as a guide only, allowing the conversation that develops to explore further the connections between the supervisees' personal and professional development and the critical ways in which their racial identity plays a part in this development.

Using cultural genograms to develop cultural sensitivity

I use the *Cultural Genogram* (Hardy and Laszloffy, 1995) as a tool with supervisees to help us explore our own cultural and racial identities to promote cultural awareness and sensitivity. I invite supervisees to draw their own family of origin genogram over three generations, annotating the diagram, to indicate their culture of origin (or, for many, the complex interweaving of cultures that are part of their heritage). I invite them to identify organising principles and pride and shame issues; those aspects of their cultures that are sanctioned as distinctly negative or positive (Hardy and Laszloffy, 1997). I share my own cultural genogram with my supervisees as part of this exercise.

This exercise has invited supervisees to reflect on their cultural assumptions and stereotypes, thereby facilitating their awareness of culturally based emotional triggers and drawing out connections between their own unique cultural identity and their therapeutic style and effectiveness (Hardy and Laszloffy, 1997). The *Cultural Genogram* exercise has also inspired discussion about the way in which culture is defined, the construction of racial identity as a part of a wider cultural identity, and how these issues have shaped the ways in which the supervisees and I think about ourselves, our families and the clients with whom we are working.

For example, my own cultural genogram identifies the way in which my sense of culture and racial identity is formed through my being brought up by my adoptive White British parents and later in life forming significant relationships with my Indian birth family. I consider my *racial* identity to be Black Indian, because my childhood experiences compelled me to confront the influence of not being White on a day-to-day basis. I consider my *cultural* identity to be largely White British, as so many of my cultural points of reference have been British over time. The pride that my adoptive family placed upon establishing and maintaining a professional career relates to the similar pride that my birth family places upon educational attainment. The influence of these aspects of my cultural and racial identity upon my clinical work are many and varied, but one particularly prominent feature is my emphasis upon the idea of cultural and racial belonging in my work with children and young people who appear to have been displaced from their own culture of origin.

In exploring racial identity within their own families, I invite supervisees to reflect on the positions of privilege and of oppression they and their family might occupy now or might have occupied in their history. I also ask them to consider how privilege and oppression might have influenced their development as clinicians. I offer, as example, my own position as a Black Indian boy growing up in a White English dominated context; and connect this position of oppression to my starting out in a career in social work focused upon working with marginalised and oppressed families.

It is the sharing of the therapists' and supervisors' own culture, racial identity and the way in which they understand and are organised by "race" and racism in their everyday lives and relationships that is the most exciting and vibrant way to dispel stereotypes and to convey the notion of cultural (and racial) diversity (Boyd-Franklin, 2003).

Talking and not talking about "race" and racism

My supervisory practice with Ruth (pp. 24–5) clearly illustrated that, despite having the commitment, knowledge and experience of talking about "race" and racism, I still did not address "race" and racism in this clinical supervision. A limited pool of research appears to confirm that my experience was not unusual; talk about "race" and racism is not usually integrated into supervision.

Lawless *et al.* (2001) undertook an exploration of how talk of "race", ethnicity and culture is accomplished within a supervision session using conversation analysis with supervisors who view these issues as being important. They found that the discourse of "race", ethnicity and culture was not held in a neat and tidy conversation, but rather had an ambiguous beginning with the talk meandering through and around other topical areas. "Race", ethnicity and culture were talked about as they connected to other clinical issues rather than being issues that were raised directly. There was not one instance found of the supervisor directly introducing these ideas into conversation.

Similarly, Hernández *et al.* (2009) in the USA explored the experiences of ethnic minority approved supervisors as supervisees in their earlier training. They found that "race" and racism appeared not to be attended to due to a lack of supervisor cultural competency, evidenced by most participants feeling that their supervisors conducted supervision from a Eurocentric perspective that denied their (racial) identities. In some cases, participants experienced overt racism from their supervisors in the form of racist comments made towards them and the matching of them therapeutically with client families of their own ethnicity. This finding of overt racism was seen to support the notion that the power differential between supervisor and supervisee is compounded when the supervisor is of a privileged racial background. This apparent power differential is of critical importance if we are to address the question of why it is that talk about "race" and racism does not appear, in practice, to be an integral part of clinical supervision.

The influence of power within the supervisory relationship

Power is embedded in the supervision relationship (Nilsson, 2007; Hernández and McDowell, 2010). In view of the evaluative dimension of supervision, a supervisee is likely to perceive the supervisor to be more expert, more experienced and to fulfil a professional gate-keeping function regarding the profession. The construction of the supervisory relationship in this way allows the supervisor to hold a position of power over the supervisee, exercising greater influence in this relationship in terms of, for instance, having their clinical views implemented by the supervisee, or ensuring that talk about "race" and racism is a central part of clinical supervision.

The increasing influence of a postmodern position within clinical practice, and particularly systemic psychotherapy, invites an alternative view of the supervisory relationship. Within a postmodern frame supervision is viewed as a collaborative conversation, with the supervisor adopting a 'not-knowing' position (Anderson and Goolishian, 1992) and engaging in co-operative meaning making with the supervisee through their talk together, in order to promote the supervisee creating their own answers to issues raised, thereby experiencing freedom and self-competence. The supervisor is not viewed as holding a position of greater authority, and so should not promote their own ideas or dominate the supervisees' ideas (Anderson and Swim, 1995). This understanding of collaborative supervision could allow talk about "race", and racism, to be left off the agenda by the supervisor.

Murphy and Wright's (2005) study, examining the use of power in the supervisory relationship, found all their supervisee participants viewed the supervisor as being in a position of power in relation to them. Further, the supervisory relationship is constructed through the dominant discourses of gender, race, religion, age, ability, class, culture, ethnicity, education, sexuality and spirituality, the *social GRRAACCEESS* (Burnham *et al.*, 2008), which serve to privilege some whilst marginalising others. This, in turn, shapes the nature of relationships and delineates what is possible (or not) within them. For example, a White, male, middle-class, heterosexual, able-bodied, well-educated supervisor might offer a tentative suggestion to a Black, female, working-class supervisee, in a desire to promote a co-constructed therapeutic intervention. This will be heard within a relationship constructed between them, in which he holds a privileged position by virtue of his supervisor status together with multiple other social locations. The possibility of the supervisee dismissing her supervisor's suggestion from the multiple marginalised positions she occupies is slight. In following his suggestion, however it is offered, the supervisor's power in their relationship is acted out (see Philip Messent's chapter 3 for further examples).

In my supervisory practice with Ruth (pp. 24–5), the power that I held as Ruth's supervisor, compounded by my privileged social location, in terms of gender and clinical experience, gave me a greater influence in our supervision conversation. In this position I was able to exclude from our conversation the influence of "race" and the possible process of racism in the family's life and in our work with them. Upon reflection, I think I was influenced in this deliberate act by my willingness to hold to a position as a collaborative supervisor, not wanting to raise these issues directly, together with feeling anxious about positioning Ruth as a clinician who does not attend to "race" and the process of racism. I did not want Ruth to think that I was identifying her or her practice as being racist. As an alternative position I might have explicitly acknowledged the power imbalance in our relationship, and exercised my power to put the idea of "race" and the process of racism on the table for discussion. Although I did not do this, one might argue that for supervisors to act ethically they should challenge inequality in these ways. Further, that it is the responsibility of the supervisor to act from their position of power and openly address the idea of "race" and the process of racism as it impacts upon the supervisory relationship and on the relationship between the therapist, supervisor and clients.

Talking about "race" and racism

The question, then, is this: as a supervisor, how might I act from my position of greater power and influence to address the idea of "race" and racism without replicating the oppressive use of power I seek to challenge or inviting the adoption of polarised positions? Returning to Ruth's supervision, I could make transparent the power associated with our different social locations by situating myself in relation to the positions from which I speak and I might attempt to mitigate the potential for oppression by joining with Ruth in a mutual sharing of experience and ideas. For instance, I might say to Ruth:

As a supervisor, I am thinking about my responsibility to consider how "race" and racism might be influencing our work with the family. I know there is a risk that addressing this might be uncomfortable for both of us. Could we take that risk and then talk about discomfort when or if it happens?

As a Black Indian man supervising a White British woman, I wonder what beliefs we may each hold about Nigerian families. Let's explore our beliefs together and think about how they might be influencing our work with the family.

As a therapist, I have worked with many Black Nigerian families and I have heard many stories about the effects of racism in their lives. If we were to consider that racism could be the experience of this family too, what ideas might we have about how you could explore that with them? How could you talk about this in a way that would fit with the concerns they are bringing to the session?

As a Black Indian man, "race" and racism have been central to my experience, and I might think that I will be much more aware of the issues of "race" and racism in the lives and relationships of the families we work with than you are. How do you think "race" and racism might have shaped your experience as a White woman, and might position you in conversations we have together about these issues? Shall we generate some ideas about how this aspect of our identities might influence us in the work; how it might influence the way the family sees us and the way in which we see each other?

Mindful of a desire to be collaborative in supervision with Ruth and not impose issues she does not raise herself, I might choose to *stay close to her concern* that she felt there was no hope for the family. I might invite her to explore this difficulty from the perspective of "race" and racism. For instance, I might say:

- 'I think "hope and hopelessness" sounds like a really important theme here and one that might make a rich contribution to the work. I wonder what it would mean to the family for their therapist to have no hope of change. If we were to imagine ourselves as a Black Nigerian family listening in to this conversation about hope, what might we say about ourselves and about the therapy?'
- 'I wonder how the family's experience of hope and hopelessness in therapy might resonate with their experience as a Black Nigerian family living in a White British majority society. If we were to explore that question in relation to the problem the family has come with, what ideas could we generate together?'
- 'Do you often feel hopeless in this way? If not, I wonder what could be making you vulnerable to hopelessness in working with this family, as I see you have been working hard to bring about change. Do you have any ideas? Thinking about aspects of social difference, do you think a White therapist working with a Black family might be more vulnerable to hopelessness? Why would that be? As a White woman, how could you challenge hopelessness in this situation? As a Black Indian man, how could I help you without reinforcing this sense of hopelessness?'

Towards an ethical supervisory practice

The idea of "race" and the process of racism organise our lives and relationships and the lives and relationships of those we meet in our clinical practice in profound ways. Therefore, it is the supervisor's responsibility to ensure that talk about "race" and racism must form a part of the very fabric of supervision, using the power inherent in their role as well as their skills as mentor, enabler, evaluator and teacher to do so.

In order to meet this responsibility, the supervisor needs to establish a relational context within which such conversations might take place. Conversations about "race" and racism are difficult and sensitive. Thus, the supervisor needs to take the lead in demonstrating critical social awareness and cultural humility, in order to develop trust and safety (Hernández and McDowell, 2010) and to establish a context in which relational risks might be taken. Hernández and Rankin (2008) describe this context as allowing students and supervisors to raise questions, challenge points of view, ponder issues, confront opinions, articulate ideas and express concerns. The development of such a relationship takes place over time. In this chapter I offer exercises to help establish a foundation for care and support while developing critical consciousness within supervision (Hernández and Rankin, 2008). In initiating these conversations the supervisor shows the acceptability of reflecting upon issues of self within the supervisory relationship and relationships with client families, and can model the taking of relational risks. The aim is to demonstrate that the idea of "race" and the process of racism matter within supervisory and therapeutic practice and to promote an ethical supervisory and clinical practice in which racial inequality is challenged rather than maintained. These conversations need to be an ongoing feature of clinical systemic supervision. The inequality between Black people and White people must continue to be challenged in this way and anything less, one might argue, is simply not good enough in the pursuit of social justice and the elimination of inequality that many practitioners and supervisors of therapy and counselling see as a central part of their work.

Note

1. Reprinted by permission of HarperCollins Publishers Ltd © (2013) (Chimamanda Ngozi Adichie)

References

Adichie, C. N. (2013) *Americanah.* Kindle Edition. London: 4th Estate.

Almeida, R., Hernández-Wolfe, P. and Tubbs, C. (2011) Cultural equity: bridging the complexity of social identities with therapeutic practices. *The International Journal of Narrative Therapy and Community Work*, 3, 43–56.

Anderson, H. and Goolishian, H. (1992) The client is the expert: a not-knowing approach to therapy. In S. McNamee and K. Gergen (eds). *Therapy as Social Construction.* London: Sage.

Anderson, H. and Swim, S. (1995) Supervision as collaborative conversation: connecting the voices of supervisor and supervisee. *Journal of Systemic Therapies*, 14(2), 1–13.

Arnold, M. S. (1993) Ethnicity and training marital and family therapists. *Counselor Education and Supervision*, 33, 139–47.

Ayo, Y. (2010) Addressing issues of race and culture in supervision. In C. Burck and G. Daniel (eds). *Mirrors and Reflections: Processes of Systemic Supervision.* London: Karnac.

BBC NEWS (2009) *Newsbeat.* [Online] Available from: www.bbc.co.uk/newsbeat/10002087. Accessed 2 November 2011.

Boyd-Franklin, N. (1989) *Black Families in Therapy.* New York: Guilford Press.

Boyd-Franklin, N. (2003) *Black Families in Therapy.* 2nd Ed. New York: Guilford Press.

Burnham, J., Alvis Palma, D. and Whitehouse, L. (2008) Learning as a context for differences and differences as a context for learning. *Journal of Family Therapy,* 30, 529–42.

Cook, D. A. (1994) Racial identity in supervision. *Counselor Education & Supervision,* 34(2), 132–41.

Count Me In 2010 census: www.cqc.org.uk/organisations-we-regulate/mental-health-services/count-me-2010-census. Accessed 18 September 2013.

Dalal, F. (2002) *Race, Colour and the Processes of Racialization.* Hove and New York: Brunner–Routledge.

Divac, A. and Heaphy, G. (2005) Space for GRAAACCES: training for cultural competence in supervision. *Journal of Family Therapy*, 27, 280–85.

Erskine, R. (2002) Exposing racism, exploring race. *Journal of Family Therapy*, 24, 282–97.

Equality and Human Rights Commission (2010) *How Fair is Britain? Equality, Human Rights and Good Relations in 2010.* London: EHRC.

Equality and Human Rights Commission (2013) *Briefing Paper 7, Race Disproportionality in Stops and Searches, 2011–12.* Manchester: EHRC.

Goldner, V. (1988) Generation and gender: normative and covert hierarchies. *Family Process*, 27, 17–31.

Gunaratnam, Y. (2003) *Researching "Race" and Ethnicity. Methods, Knowledge and Power.* London: Sage.

Hardy, K. V. (2008) Race, reality and relationships: implications for the re-visioning of family therapy. In M. McGoldrick and K. V. Hardy (eds). *Re-Visioning Family Therapy.* 2nd Ed. New York: Guilford Press.

Hardy, K. V. and Laszloffy, T. A. (1995) The cultural genogram: key to training culturally competent family therapists. *Journal of Marital and Family Therapy*, 21(3), 227–37.

Hardy, K. V. and Laszloffy, T. A. (1997) An application of the cultural genogram in supervision. In T. Todd and C. Storm (eds). *The Complete Systemic Supervisor Resource Guide.* Boston: Allyn and Bacon.

Hardy, K. V. and Laszloffy, T. A. (2000) Uncommon strategies for a common problem: addressing racism in family therapy. *Family Process*, 39, 35–50.

Hare-Mustin, R. (1978) A feminist approach to family therapy. *Family Process*, 17, 181–94.

Hernández, P., Taylor, B. A. and McDowell, T. (2009) Listening to ethnic minority AAMFT approved supervisors: reflections on their experiences as supervisees. *Journal of Systemic Therapies*, 28(1), 88–100.

Hernández, P. and McDowell, T. (2010) Intersectionality, power, and relational safety in context: key concepts in clinical supervision. *Training and Education in Professional Psychology*, 4(1), 29–35.

Hernández, P. and Rankin, P. (2008) Relational safety in supervision. *Journal of Marital and Family Therapy*, 34, 58–74.

James, K. and McIntyre, D. (1983) The reproduction of families: the social role of family therapy? *Journal of Marital and Family Therapy*, 9, 119–29.

Lawless, J. J., Gale, J. E. and Bacigalupe, G. (2001) The discourse of race and culture in family therapy supervision: a conversational analysis. *Contemporary Family Therapy,* 23(2), 181–97.

Mason, B. (2005) Relational risk-taking and the training of supervisors. *Journal of Family Therapy*, 27, 298–301.

McGoldrick, M. (ed.) (1998) *Re-Visioning Family Therapy.* New York: Guilford Press.
McGoldrick, M. and Hardy, K. V. (2008) Introduction: re-visioning family therapy from a multicultural perspective. In M. McGoldrick and K. V. Hardy (eds). *Re-Visioning Family Therapy.* 2nd Ed. New York: Guilford Press.
Miller, D., Coleman, J., Connolly, W. and Ryan, A. (eds) (1987) *The Blackwell Encyclopaedia of Political Thought.* Oxford: WileyBlackwell.
Ministry of Justice (2008) Ministry of Justice, statistics on race and the criminal justice system 2006–7. www.justice.gov.uk/publications/statistics.htm
Murphy, M. and Wright, D. (2005) Supervisees' perspectives of power use in supervision. *Journal of Marital and Family Therapy*, 31(3), 283–95.
Nilsson, J. (2007) International students in supervision. *The Clinical Supervisor*, 26(1), 35–47.
Pendry, N. (2012) Race, racism and systemic supervision. *Journal of Family Therapy*, 34, 403–18.
Reach Report (2007) www.communities.gov.uk/publications/communities/reachreport.
Renn, K. A. (2012) Creating and re-creating race: the emergence of racial identity as a critical element in psychological, sociological, and ecological perspectives on human development. In C. J. Wijeyesinghe and B. W. Jackson III (eds). *New Perspectives on Racial Identity Development.* 2nd Ed. New York and London: New York University Press.
Singh, R. (2009) Constructing 'the family' across culture. *Journal of Family Therapy*, 31, 359–83.
Smedley, A. and Smedley, B. D. (2005) Race as biology is fiction, racism as social problem is real: anthropological and historical perspectives on the social construction of race. *American Psychologist*, 60, 16–26.
Solomos, J. (2003) *Race and Racism in Britain.* 3rd Ed. Hampshire: Palgrave Macmillan.
Tatum, B. D. (1997) *Why are All the Black Kids Sitting Together in the Cafeteria?* New York: Basic Books.
Totsuka, Y. (2014) 'Which aspects of social GGRRAAACCEEESSS grab you most?' The social GGRRAAACCEEESSS exercise for a supervision group to promote therapists' self-reflexivity. *Journal of Family Therapy*, 36, 86–106. doi: 10.1111/1467-6427.12026
Zephaniah, B. (2012) www.theguardian.com/commentisfree/video/2012/oct/01/benjamin-zephaniah-poetry-video. Accessed 18 September 2013.

3 Supervision across ethnic difference

Learning of a White supervisor and manager

Philip Messent

In Antonioni's film *The Passenger* (1975) Jack Nicholson plays Mr Locke, a rather jaded journalist interviewing a revolutionary African leader. He asks this imposing and enigmatic African man a string of questions about his motivation and the effects of a period of time he spent in Europe.

> After a pause, the leader replies crisply and assertively: 'Mr Locke, there are perfectly satisfactory answers to all your questions. But I don't think you understand how little you can learn from them. Your questions are much more revealing about yourself than my answers would be about me'. The journalist replies earnestly: 'I mean them quite sincerely'. The leader replies: 'Mr Locke, we can have a conversation – but only if it's not just what *you* think is sincere, but also what *I* believe to be honest'. With this the leader gets up and takes charge of the camera, which up until this moment has been pointed at him, swivelling it round so that it is now filming the rather bewildered looking Mr Locke, and says: 'Now we can have an interview. . .'.

Echoing the perspective of the African leader in this film clip (quoted by di Nicola, 1997), Gill Gorrell Barnes (2002) notes that 'In writing about ethnicity at all, one of the traps for white Anglo-Saxon English people is to think first about other, rather than self' (p. 134). In this chapter I try to turn the camera on myself, a White, male, English, middle-class family therapist and supervisor, senior both in years and in my profession. Through conversations with supervisees of different ethnicities, I describe my learning about supervision across ethnic difference with examples from my practice as a supervisor within child and adolescent mental health public services, where I have been responsible for offering both clinical and management supervision. I draw on examples from my supervisory practice over a 25-year period, from my early experiences of supervising trainees in placements to offering different kinds of clinical supervision to qualified practitioners, including live supervision in the room or behind a one-way screen, individual or group reflective supervision, and also managerial supervision that requires monitoring the performance of clinical practitioners to meet targets.

I believe that we bring to every encounter our culture, values and histories which we embody in our very presence. Our gender, age, class, sexuality and religion shape how we embody our race and inform the questions we ask and the answers we hear. Therefore, in my attempt to establish more 'honest' relationships, over the years I have moved from trying to learn all I can about the cultures of people with whom I am working (Messent, 1992) to starting to examine the part that my whiteness plays in my interactions with clients and other workers of different cultures (Messent, 2004; Hernández and McDowell, 2010).

When I spoke with a supervisee from an ethnicity different from my own about my personal shift, she said (optimistically) that this sort of cross-cultural supervision could 'add colour' to the supervision, 'enrich it with a diversity' and 'add to the complexity' of what could be discussed between us. In this chapter I explore how to maximise the possibility of such a mutually enriching 'colouring' within supervision. Mindful of the risk that I might diminish or silence the voice of ethnic minority supervisees, I also consider how I can speak from my supervisory and management positions of power and knowledge in a way that avoids colonising practices.

Lessons from co-working across difference

Often in our professional roles in the public health service we share tasks with other workers like co-working with a client, joint teaching or working collaboratively on a service development. Liz Burns and Charmaine Kemps (2002), two women colleagues, one of European-English origin, the other of Asian origin, describe the process of preparing together a conference presentation on cross-cultural working. They found that they were often faced with the dilemma of speaking their minds at the risk of upsetting or offending the other, with the consequences of their communications being 'painfully unpredictable' (p. 149). Their learning from some of the challenges and discomfort they experienced in negotiating aspects of their difference, offers useful application to supervision across difference.

Burns and Kemps describe how they managed working together, despite discomfort in recognising their difference in perspectives. They found that acknowledging and sharing their own vulnerabilities and showing they were able to hear alternative perspectives and respond to them, made an important contribution to 'maintaining open communication and greater understanding without either (of us) abandoning dignity and a sense of identity' (p. 155). In the light of their experience they offer some guiding principles for co-workers from different cultures embarking upon similar ventures:

- Be aware (and beware!) of assumptions and presumptions in the context of shared projects.
- Be prepared for unpredictable differences that may take you by surprise. They are likely to be deeply embedded in past professional, personal, family, social, political and cultural experiences and to be emotionally loaded.

- Be prepared to take risks in confronting the discomfort and disagreement together if you want to explore greater depths.
- Make an agreement about how you will communicate with each other if there are feelings of hurt and misunderstanding.

My colleagues and I (Anane-Agyei *et al.*, 2002) describe experiences similar to Burns and Kemps of misunderstanding and discomfort between us whilst establishing an African Families Service. From our learning we generated additional guiding principles that enabled us to work with 'honesty', 'enriching our practice with diversity' by 'adding colour' and 'complexity' including:

- Creating space to explore the impact of cross-cultural mistrust and negative judgements on relationships between workers.
- Considering involving a third party facilitator to help us.
- Keeping the focus on the outcomes of our work with clients.
- Reflecting on the effect of our relationships on the work.
- Hearing different viewpoints without polarisation.
- Acknowledging and witnessing best intentions towards each other.

> In our African Families project, a White worker and a Black African worker always worked together alongside each other on every case. On one occasion a White worker took a back seat during the interview, intending to demonstrate respect for her Black colleague's particular expertise in this area. Later the White worker learned that the Black worker had experienced her sitting back as being 'left to do all the work' while the White worker 'sat back in judgement'.

Through careful discussion, the White worker in the above description was helped to recognise and understand why her Black colleague had experienced her 'sitting back' as 'judgement' when her colleague generously disclosed many examples in which previously she had been placed 'without negotiation' in positions of responsibility for pieces of work and then critically evaluated by other White colleagues and managers. The workers invited a trusted colleague to act as a facilitator agreeing that time would need to be set aside to reach an understanding about what had gone wrong between them. In this space of relational safety (Hernández and Rankin, 2008) in which both workers could look at their 'assumptions and presumptions' and take risks to 'confront discomfort', the White worker learned the importance of clarifying her intentions and negotiating different positions in the work (for example, interviewer or team) rather than assuming that her intentions would be automatically understood.

Learning through supervision across difference

I will now return to the supervision context in which similar misunderstandings can arise between supervisors and supervisees of different ethnicities. Since our ways of understanding our encounters are informed by the different perspectives born not only of our cultures and personal histories, but also our positions in professional hierarchies, in supervision we have the added challenge of negotiating difference in power and status. My learning in this area has often occurred when something has 'felt wrong' to me – either a supervisee has demonstrated some degree of discomfort, or I have felt some sense of unease in an encounter, or there has been some sort of internal conflict for me between several competing principles.

Kimmel (2014) has compared the position of being White, male and heterosexual to running 'with the wind at your back'; from this position we only rarely realise how we are sustained, supported and propelled by that wind. It is at moments of discomfort that my attention is most likely to be drawn to the difference that my position of privilege brings to my encounters.

Attending to bodily positioning

> A White, Irish female trainee went very silent and unresponsive during a reflective supervision session when I tried to elucidate a theoretical point by drawing a diagram on a whiteboard. Later, in the context of a three-way meeting with her college tutor, she told me that she experienced me as 'superior' and 'school-masterly' which 'disempowered' and 'silenced' her.

I had used the whiteboard as an aid to elucidate a complex issue assuming this would be for our mutual benefit. I had seen myself as attempting to equalise relationships in the way that I had been talking with her, not as adopting any sort of superior stance. Therefore, it came as a shock to hear that I had been experienced as 'school-masterly'. I had not thought about how an educative stance on the part of a White, English, middle-class supervisor who was an older man, in a position of power and influence, might be experienced. This experience taught me to be mindful of the effects of how I position my body, of when and how to use teaching aids, such as whiteboards, and the need to contextualise practices within supervision. Since then, I take the time to check with supervisees if it would be useful for me to write things down. I also explain that I find it a helpful way of clarifying my thinking and express my hope that it might be useful for the supervisee as well. Instead of standing up and writing on a board at some distance, thereby embodying the position of an educator who has to be looked up to, I offer to sit alongside the supervisee, a piece of paper between us, inviting him or her to contribute so we both can add to the 'picture' we are discussing. In this way, I hope to use my bodily positioning to invite supervisees' collaboration in moving towards a shared understanding and way forward. I have not completely abandoned using the whiteboard in supervision. However, I am mindful of its potential for entrenching power differentials and silencing supervisees, and now check in more carefully with supervisees about its impact and usefulness.

> A female Asian supervisee told me that all of her supervisors (up to and including me) had been White men and all had sat in supervision meetings with her on chairs that were higher than hers, and that had higher and more imposing backs.

It took her generous act in pointing this out for me to realise the significance of this difference in bodily positioning and, since then, to re-think the way that I use seating arrangements.

Welcoming difference

Another learning experience, for me as a supervisor, was with my very first trainee from a Bangladeshi background. I felt that it was a very important first step for our service as a whole to offer placements to Bangladeshi trainees, since an increasing proportion of the population in the service's catchment area had their origins in Bangladesh, but were only minimally represented within our specialist work force. I was anxious that my colleagues and managers saw the placement as successful and perceived the trainee as 'fitting in', as I hoped the success of this placement would lay the ground for recruiting Bangladeshi practitioners into substantive posts in the future.

> The trainee's first client was a White, working-class family. I was providing supervision from behind a one-way screen, from where I witnessed the trainee greeting the family into the room with (to my White Anglo-Saxon eyes) 'over-effusive' thanks for their attendance, pleasure about meeting them, and close attention to their needs for their coats to be taken off and securely hung up. My feeling about this greeting at the time was one of discomfort and disapproval. I felt that the trainee was giving a message contrary to the prevalent view in the service at that time – that practitioners in our service should convey a neutral message to client-families about whether to take up the offer of help rather than encourage them to attend. 'Tone down your pleasure about their attendance', I told my trainee, explaining the service's prevalent stance towards clients coming to the service.

I could see in his subsequent meetings with families that the trainee was making attempts to rein in his style of making families feel welcome, becoming more subdued and less effusive in the way that he greeted them. Over time, I realised that my instructions were unhelpfully undermining what was an important part of his cultural repertoire for making connections with people. Therefore, I desisted from further attempts to encourage him to 'fit in' with what I realised was a particularly White and middle-class style of greeting.

Looking back now, I see this episode as similar to the Just Therapy team's early attempts to introduce workers from the Maori and Pacific Island communities to a team that, until that point, had been largely White (Waldegrave, 1994). The institution wanted to integrate a different (non-white) perspective, but when this brought with it more difference than existing staff were ready for (like a new worker introducing the practice of the staff group sharing lunches every day), the original White team felt discomforted. My trainee was behaving in ways that were initially too different from our service's particular way of greeting clients, although over time I was able to appreciate his intention, and indeed the benevolent effect of these greetings, since clients' responses demonstrated that they liked to be made welcome in this way.

Learning from this experience has led me to invite trainees and supervisees to mutually share our different cultural styles of greeting and the intentions informing our practices, rather than attempt to impose the prevailing culture of the institution as the 'correct' way of doing things. For example, I might say something like, 'Some of us in the clinic shake hands when we meet a family for the first time, whereas others think this is too familiar. How do you prefer to greet people you meet for the first time?' 'How does this fit with your usual cultural ways of greeting?' 'Is it the same with men/women/children?' I also invite reflection on how they are likely to be received by others from different cultures, for example, 'Some people describe my style as "English reserve". How do you see it?' 'How do you think [this client] would prefer to be welcomed?'

Mindful of the way in which minority cultures and practices will often be labelled as deviant and inferior (see Afuape, chapter 7, this volume), I recognise the need for me, as a White, male supervisor, to 'continually interrogate my participation in the colonial project' (Hernández and McDowell, 2010: 31) ensuring that I am appreciating multiple and especially marginalised viewpoints and expressions. It is often through our bodies that our cultural affiliations are enacted: in what our bodies *do*, as in different styles of greeting, and in what our bodies *show* as in, for instance, different styles of dress. Our age, gender, culture and religion all influence the way we dress and present ourselves.

A Black male supervisee of Asian heritage regularly sported long hair and multiple earrings. My first instinct in the past had been to suggest that supervisees dress to conform more to the dominant 'professional' code. I have realised that to ask them to 'tone down' their appearance is to act anew as a coloniser, requiring them to conform to the dominant cultural way. This risks undermining their position and diminishing the opportunity of their bringing a different way of being which might enrich the work we are doing together. Therefore, I use versions of the questions above to invite a mutual exploration of our different styles of dress and presentation (theirs and mine), and invite reflection on how the people with whom we work might experience and respond to our different styles.

Similarities, differences and intersecting identities

When supervising across ethnic difference, there are a number of different possibilities with regard to the similarities and differences between the client, supervisee and supervisor. For example, figure 3.1a reflects the difference–similarity

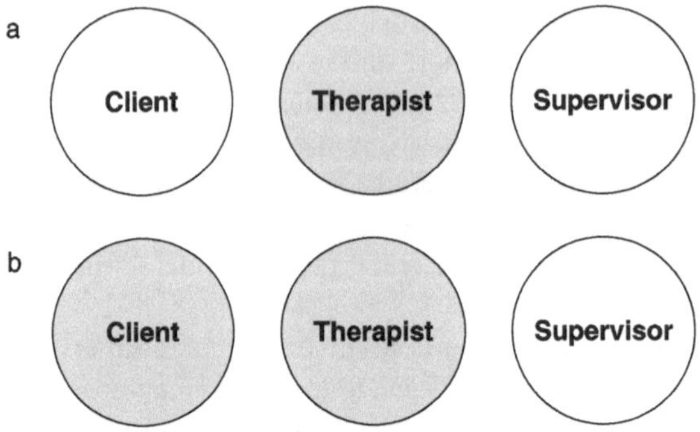

Figure 3.1 Similarities and differences in supervision

constellation in supervision with my Bangladeshi trainee, where the supervisor and client-family belong to the same dominant ethnic group and the therapist/supervisee to the minority ethnic group. In figure 3.1b the supervisor is of the dominant ethnic group and both the therapist/supervisee and the client-family of the same minority ethnic group.

The balance of assumed knowledge and authority to speak differ in these different situations. When I started supervising the Bangladeshi trainee, I was assuming that, as a member of the same ethnic group as the White client-family (figure 3.1a) I was more expert than the Bangladeshi supervisee about the style of encounter with which the client would be comfortable. I also positioned myself as the expert on how greetings and welcome were usually conducted in the institution. Assuming this expert position, however, I disregarded other differences and similarities between the client-family and me and between the supervisee and me. For example, the client-family belonged to a different class and socio-economic group from me (that was more similar to the supervisee's), so in no way could I be considered an expert on their culture and what would make them comfortable in coming to this service. In fact, my supervisee's warmth elicited an openness and sense of ease in their encounter across ethnic difference which took me by surprise.

The therapist/supervisee in figure 3.1b is likely to have a great deal of local knowledge about the community she shares with the client, such as the ways in which families behave, what they believe, how they solve problems, their values and so on. Therefore, the supervisee might assume or be allocated a position of cultural 'expert' and expected to inform or educate the dominant culture supervisor. One possible problem with this positioning is that it can place too much of an onus on the supervisee to be the expert on the local community as though they can or even should know everything there is to know about their community's culture. We might say that the White colleague (discussed on p. 36) who 'took a back seat', in respect for her Black colleague's 'expertise in this area', positioned her colleague as cultural expert without discussion or negotiation.

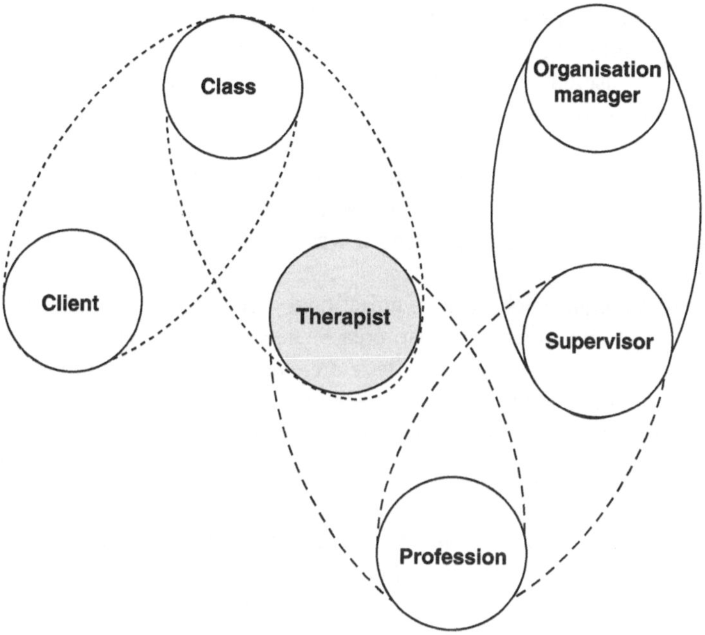

Figure 3.2 Multiple intersecting identities in supervision

Positioning people as cultural experts on the basis of their membership of a particular ethnic group suggests a view of culture as a fixed and static entity that people belong to or not. We have learnt, however, (di Nicola, 1997) to see culture as ever-changing.

Since we have loyalties to several different cultures at once, we need a more complex model reflecting that supervisor and supervisee can belong to multiple contexts. Figure 3.2 takes into account the multiple intersecting identities that we may prioritise or foreground at different times. For example, in figure 3.1a (p. 40) I, the supervisor, share the same race and culture (White English identity) with the client-family; the Bangladeshi therapist/supervisee has a loyalty to and historical origins situated in the same class (working-class identity) as the family; the supervisee shares a loyalty with me to our professional community (social worker identity) that he has recently joined. I also hold line management responsibility (manager identity) for the supervisee.

Analysing the impact of intersecting identities

Hernández and McDowell (2010) suggest that 'analysing the impact of intersecting identities' can contribute to the process of 'critical postcolonial supervision'. It was a complex intersection of gender, age, class, structural inequality and colonial history that contributed to the interaction between the female Irish trainee and myself going wrong. Where an age difference is involved, alongside a gender and ethnicity difference, the possibilities for making sense of the mis-understandings and things going wrong are multiplied. As older supervisors we are not always conscious of the difference that our perceived age makes to the way in which our actions or perspectives are experienced. My age possibly added to the trainee's experience of me as 'school-masterly' and made it more difficult for what went wrong to be voiced. Addressing the ways in which our identities intersected, with the help of a third party, enabled us to understand the powerful feelings that had been evoked, and find a way of going on in our supervisory relationship.

Sometimes the requirements the organisational system places upon us as managers, supervisors and supervisees can create tensions in our relationships. For example, in the public health service, there are ever-increasing requirements for managers to monitor and hold supervisees accountable for the quantity and quality of work undertaken, with growing amounts of data routinely collected for this purpose.

> In supervision, I raised a series of issues connected with volume and recording of work with a Black female supervisee with whom I had enjoyed, what I thought of as, a friendly and open relationship over a number of years. In our discussion I offered suggestions about how she could better represent herself and her work in a way that, I thought, offered guidance about navigating the challenges of the organisational system of which we were both a part. However, the supervisee received my communication as critical, undermining of her position and intimating that she was not working hard enough. We were both very distressed about this apparent breakdown in our mutual trust and respect and, after some days, agreed that we needed to meet again to discuss what had happened and to find a way of going on.
>
> With great generosity and forbearance, my supervisee explained the impact upon her of my raising a sequence of issues regarding her 'performance', and I was able to recognise that, with hindsight, my raising these issues in a single meeting had had the cumulative effect of positioning me as critical and fault-finding.

Analysing our intersecting identities, we could see that our gender and ethnic differences and the different positions we held in the organisational hierarchy contributed to the way that things had gone wrong between us. Naming these differences seemed to render them less powerful in their effects, opening space for us to spend some time reflecting on the rights, duties and responsibilities given us by our different positions in the hierarchy and the impact of our respective genders and ethnicity on how we experienced these differences.

Speaking with different voices

The process of analysing our intersecting identities brought into view the multiple contexts out of which I was acting with my supervisee. These included our clinical supervision relationship; my clinical service team where I held a lead clinician responsibility; the service management group of the organisation; and our shared family therapy profession. Each context shaped and informed my different identities in our working relationship. Naming my different 'selves' of 'supervisor', 'manager' and 'mentor' in our working relationship, opened space for me to talk with my supervisee from the different contexts or positions out of which I was acting (Martin and Stott, 2010).

> Therefore I went on, 'If I speak with my manager voice (while listening to my own manager talking in my right ear) I would be discussing with you about the need to prioritise case throughput and proposing that you close this case now. On the other hand, if I speak with my mentor voice I would have your professional development in mind and would see you continuing to work with this interesting case as more important. How can we do justice to both these voices?'

Naming my different identities or 'selves' and speaking with different voices helped the supervisee and me move into a more fruitful discussion about the constraints we both faced working for an organisation with limited resources.

Richards (2002) describes how, as a Black worker presenting a cultural perspective on the use of physical punishment of children within some Black families, she risks being identified by colleagues as supporting the beliefs that physical punishment of children is justified and hence being seen as 'unprofessional' (p. 121). Inviting supervisees to speak from the different contexts informing their identities has enabled supervisees to share their cultural perspectives without compromising their sense of professional integrity.

> In a reflective practice supervision group with me, Bangladeshi social workers described several occasions when they felt unable to present their perspectives about their Bangladeshi clients' strengths to White managers for fear of being seen as 'over-identifying' with the clients and as 'unprofessional' (Messent, 2013). This was particularly challenging when White colleagues reported concerns about safety and were considering going to court to request care orders.

With a specific example from their practice, I invited the social workers to 'talk with your different voices, from your different positions' with questions like:

- Talking from the position of social worker: What would you say/think? What do you recommend?

- Talking with your voice of a Bangladeshi man/woman/mother: What are your views? What ideas do you have? What would you like to see happen?

Speaking from both their identities (as members of the Bangladeshi community and professional social workers), the supervisees were able to identify and name their different positions, to voice their different perspectives and to identify tensions between the positions and perspectives. We went on to explore *how* they could voice their different observations with professional and cultural integrity. From this discussion, this group decided to use the format of an 'assessment report' in which to report problems and family strengths and to demonstrate how they were taking account of both to inform decisions.

Developing relational safety in supervision

'Relational safety' between supervisor and supervisee is a key ingredient of enabling critical postcolonial supervision (Hernández and McDowell, 2010). Supervisees and I have been able to address what had gone wrong between us and the part that our ethnic, gender and hierarchical differences have played when we have created a context of relational safety and a space for careful reflection. The guiding principles I describe in this chapter, summarised in the conclusion, have facilitated building relational safety. For example, the supervisee and I (above) had spoken previously about the way in which our ethnic and gender differences had the potential to undermine our attempts to collaborate and had found a way through similar difficulties in the past. Each of us had a sense of the other as well-intentioned with a shared commitment to avoiding any practices that undermined or diminished black perspectives, and to the delivery of a high-quality service for our client-families. This shared history helped us towards the relational safety necessary to find a way of going on which honoured both the work the supervisee was doing and our organisation's need to demonstrate, through its data collection, the service that was being delivered.

This was not the case with the Irish trainee and me or for the White colleague, who was experienced as 'sitting back in judgement' by the Black African practitioner. In both those situations we drew on the help of a facilitating third person to enable us to build a context of relational safety within which to explore our differences and common commitments.

> In group supervision, a Black female practitioner described difficulties making her voice heard in a school where she was attempting to argue on behalf of a Black family who, she felt, were being unfairly treated by staff at the school. I mentioned that when another practitioner (who the supervisee knew was also Black) and I visited schools together in these situations, our advice was much more impactful (Messent, 2004). The supervisee responded that she did not need the support of a 'White master' to make her voice heard. I took this as indicating that she could

> not see how I could lend my male, white and managerial voice to her and her client's cause without herself feeling positioned as subjugated. For my part, positioned as a 'White master', I was unsure how to offer any other suggestions lest they be experienced in a similar way as subjugating. As I had not negotiated with the group how we could communicate when there were feelings of hurt or misunderstanding between us, and because I did not have a shared history with this supervisee, we did not have the 'relational safety' to make sense of what had gone wrong in our interaction and to find another way of helping with the supervisory impasse.

The dilemma for White supervisors in these sorts of situations is that, by resorting to the familiar practice of benevolently using the power of our senior position to advocate for supervisees and their clients, we may find ourselves promoting a pro-racist ideology in which we are listened to because we are White rather than because we are senior. But if we hold back from using our power, we could be denying supervisees and clients the support which could make a real difference. In a context of relational safety, it would have been more possible to explore these dilemmas and come to a way forward, which ensured that both Black supervisee and White supervisor's expertise and authority were voiced in the interest of the client's well-being in the school.

Looking back, I wonder if we could have made creative use of this moment of 'relational danger'. Finding myself entered into a discourse of racism (as a 'White master') I was anxious not to step further into this identity and to retreat to safer territory, even if that meant I could not help the supervisee. I wonder what would have happened if I had lingered a little in the dangerous territory, exploring with the supervisee and group whether this powerful evocation of a discourse of racism could illuminate something about the experience of the family, worker and school. Perhaps by taking the risk to deepen discussion, as Burns and Kemps (2002) recommend, we might have begun to build the shared history that is a foundation of relational safety.

Talking about supervision experience and preferred learning styles

McCann (2000) differentiates between two different styles of supervision, the one more *directive* (for example, 'I want you to greet families less effusively') and the other more *collaborative* (for example, 'Let's think together about different ways of greeting families and what is likely to be a good fit between you and the family you are about to meet').[1] He suggests that therapists in the early stage of training benefit more from a high degree of direction from the supervisor and that a more collaborative style is only appropriate as they gain in confidence when they are ready to find their own unique style and approach. In this chapter I have shown that when supervising across ethnic difference, if we apply this rule of thumb without reaching an agreement first about how to work together, there is a risk that direction we offer may be experienced as a colonising practice and our attempts to collaboratively construct a way forward together may be experienced by an ethnic minority supervisee trying to find his or her way in a new working context as a lack of guidance and support.

Therefore, I try to begin all new supervision relationships with talking about preferred styles of learning: seeking to avoid any echoes of previously unhelpful supervisory experiences, agreeing the kind and style of supervision input that is going to be most helpful, and creating the sort of ground rules and contract for working recommended by Down (2000). This might include, for example, an agreement about how agendas for supervisory meetings are to be generated together, how decisions will be recorded, how feedback is to be given and how we will differentiate between issues where we are reflecting and co-evolving a way forward in the *domain of explanation*, and issues where potential actions are more constrained, such as the need to notify others of Child Protection concerns in the *domain of production* (see Lang *et al.*, 1990; Bond, chapter 4, this volume). As managerial supervisor, I see it as my responsibility to reach an agreement early in the supervisory process about models of supervision, and what is going to be a good fit for my supervisee, and to ensure that we regularly review the ways we are working together. Included in this conversation will be raising our cultural/ethnic (and sometimes gender, age, sexuality, class and (dis)ability) difference and the potential of my 'getting things wrong', and I encourage my supervisee to let me know of any discomfort arising in response to my ideas or ways of working. I encourage new trainees and members of staff to feel that they have valued areas of knowledge and experience to bring to the supervision meetings, and that the process of joining the organisation is not one of being assimilated and obliterating their difference. I am explicit about expecting and hoping that their different perspectives and ways of doing things will add to and enrich the culture of the institution, and that they will be contributing to the thinking and decision-making about ways of working with clients. At the same time I also clarify lines of accountability, how responsibility for decisions taken are shared and where the 'buck stops' so that they are aware of how others will see themselves as entitled and required to contribute to such decisions.

I have increasingly recognised over time the need to prepare teams and institutional contexts for the difference that ethnic minority supervisees are likely to offer. It is not enough for me, as their supervisor, to be cautious about my own colonising practices if the team of which we are both a part behaves in a way that is undermining of the difference their presence provides. (See Miller, 2002, for a discussion of preparing an institution for the difference that ethnic minority staff will offer.)

Conclusion

In this chapter I reflect on what I have learned about how, as a White supervisor and manager, I might work in supervision with practitioners from ethnic groups different from my own with the sort of 'honesty' required by the African leader quoted in *The Passenger*. Practices which are likely to be helpful include:

- Making sure the organisation is welcoming, appreciative and facilitative of learning and development for all, especially for staff and students of minority groups, while appreciating that staff from minority ethnic groups will bring with them learning for the organisation.
- Creating a supervision contract between supervisor and supervisee agreeing how we work together to establish the conditions for relational safety that include transparency about models of supervision, accountability and an agreement about how any relational discomfort between us will be addressed.
- Recognising the potential for misunderstandings resulting in things going wrong when supervising across ethnic difference, and the way in which this potential is multiplied when other differences, such as gender and age, are added.
- In considering supervisory dilemmas, broadening the context to think about different identities, contexts and positions that supervisor and supervisee may be speaking from.
- Always taking a stance which assumes good intent and capability on the part of the other.
- When supervisory relationships reach an impasse, taking time and care to seek a way to go on together, recognising underlying complexities. This will require a safe relational space to make sense together of what underlies the impasse, and may be facilitated by a mutually agreed facilitating third party.

To paraphrase von Foerster (1972), let us all (and most of all those of us in positions of greater power) take responsibility for the worlds we construct together, building through such inter-ethnic supervisory relationships the kind of organisations and world that we wish to be a part of.

Acknowledgement

I wish to acknowledge the numerous and generous contributions made to my learning by students, co-workers and supervisees in the East London NHS Foundation Trust and elsewhere.

Note

1 My examples.

References

Anane-Agyei, A., Lobatto W. and Messent, P. (2002) The African Families project: a black and white issue. In B. Mason and A. Sawyerr (eds). *Exploring the Unsaid: Creativity, Risks, and Dilemmas in Working Cross-Culturally.* London: Karnac.

The Passenger (1975) Film. Directed by M. Antonioni. Metro-Goldwyn-Mayer.

Burns, L. and Kemps, C. (2002) Risky business: the rewards and demands of cross-cultural working with colleagues. In B. Mason and A. Sawyerr (eds). *Exploring the Unsaid: Creativity, Risks, and Dilemmas in Working Cross-Culturally.* London: Karnac.

di Nicola, V. (1997) *A Stranger in the Family: Culture, Families and Therapy.* New York: Norton.

Down, G. (2000) Supervision in a multicultural context. In G. Gorrell Barnes, G. Down and D. McCann (eds). *Systemic Supervision: A Portable Guide for Supervision Training.* London: Kingsley.

Gorrell Barnes, G. (2002) Getting it right, getting it wrong: developing an internal discourse about ethnicity and difference. In B. Mason and A. Sawyerr (eds). *Exploring the Unsaid: Creativity, Risks and Dilemmas in Working Cross-Culturally.* London: Karnac.

Hernández, P. and Rankin, P. (2008) Relational safety in supervision. *Journal of Marital and Family Therapy*, 34, 58–74.

Hernández, P. and McDowell, T. (2010) Intersectionality, power and relational safety in context: key concepts in clinical supervision. *Training and Education in Professional Psychology*, 4(1), 29–35.

Kimmel, M. (2014) Introduction: towards a sociology of the superordinate. In M. Kimmel and A. Ferber (eds). *Privilege: A Reader.* 3rd Ed. Philadelphia: Westview.

Lang, P., Little, M. and Cronen, V. (1990) The systemic professional: domains of action and the question of neutrality. *Human Systems: The Journal of Systemic Consultation and Management*, 1, 39–56.

Martin, E. and Stott, J. (2010). Using our selves in work with older people. In G. Fredman, E. Anderson and J. Stott (eds). *Being with Older People: A Systemic Approach.* London: Karnac.

McCann, D. (2000) From here to eternity and back again: developing a supervisory relationship with training family therapists. In G. Gorrell Barnes, G. Down and D. McCann (eds). *Systemic Supervision: A Portable Guide for Supervision Training.* London: Kingsley.

Messent, P. (1992) Working with Bangladeshi families in the East End of London. *Journal of Family Therapy*, 14, 287–305.

Messent, P. (2004) Ethnic minority children and families: preventative approaches. In K. Dwivedi and P. Harper (eds). *Promoting the Emotional Well-being of Children and Adolescents and Preventing their Mental Ill Health.* London: Kingsley.

Miller, A. (2002) Changing the face of the organisation: addressing the challenges of work in a multi-ethnic setting. *Journal of Family Therapy*, 24, 72–84.

Richards, R. (2002) A risky balance: striving to merge professional white issues and personal black issues. In B. Mason and A. Sawyerr (eds). *Exploring the Unsaid: Creativity, Risks, and Dilemmas in Working Cross-culturally.* London: Karnac.

von Foerster, H. (1972) Responsibilities of competence. *Journal of Cybernetics*, 2(2), 1–6.

Waldegrave, C. (1994) Conference Presentation. Regent's Park College, London.

4 Supervision as a cluster of conversations

Sharon Bond

I have been developing the ideas presented in this chapter over many years in my practice as a therapist, consultant and supervisor using a systemic and social constructionist framework. To give a context to my working practice, I have been self-employed for many years. From this position I have supervised trainees to support their learning in systemic and social constructionist approaches and I have consulted to qualified professionals experienced in this approach and to practitioners interested to learn more about this way of working.

Supervision commonly focuses on client–therapist and/or therapist–supervisor relationships. In this chapter, I approach supervision as 'a social act that can be understood as the nexus (*or cluster*) of intertwined (*or overlapping*) conversations' (Pearce, 1995: 8). This cluster of conversations not only includes talks between client and therapist and therapist and supervisor but also pays attention to a multitude of 'overlapping' conversations with and between, for example, the supervisor's, supervisee's and client's family, friends, employers, community and government – all with different expectations and different degrees of influence. I aim to acknowledge and make visible some of the myriad voices that are part of these clusters of conversation we call supervision; and to explore how to invite and embody them within the process of supervision.

Starting from the position that we are embodied beings, embedded in shifting social worlds, I introduce Lang *et al.'s* (1990) theory of 'Domains of Action', which offers a way of structuring and organising supervision conversations in three domains: *production*, *explanation* and *aesthetics*. I go on to identify a fourth domain, which I have named *rhetoric*. In this domain the task is one of developing our abilities to be self-reflexive. Here we explore how our emotions and bodily responses influence the process of accountability. I hope that this chapter will offer a practical means for entering and opening space for different and varied conversations in supervision using Domains of Action theory as it is extended to include the domain of *rhetoric*.

Approaching supervision as a cluster of conversations

The Oxford Popular Dictionary (1990: 164) defines 'conversation' as 'the informal exchange of ideas by spoken words'. Pearce (1994) reminds us that conversations are more than just an exchange of ideas since they also include the ways we *do* interpersonal communication. He quotes Postman, who uses the word 'conversation' to refer 'not only to speech but to all techniques and technologies that permit people of a particular culture to exchange messages. In this sense all culture is a conversation or, more precisely, a corporation of conversations, conducted in a variety of symbolic modes' (Postman, 1985: 6, cited in Pearce, 1994: 1).

When we interact with each other, we are engaged in many complex actions that include our bodies, our feelings and our thoughts. Postman (1985) and Pearce (1994) remind us that conversations are relational and never finished, but always emerging as one conversation overlaps with another, foregrounding certain bolder voices and stories and moving others into the shadow as we create, shape, re-create and re-shape our culture. Therefore supervision takes place in a cluster of conversations in which some conversations are *bolder* than others, in the sense that they command our attention and assume an entitlement to be listened to. For example, we expect to listen to the voice of the employer or training institution that is commissioning supervision. These voices are *bold* in comparison with, for instance, the voices of the supervisee's family. Her family's opinions and concerns may be part of the cluster of conversations influencing the supervisee, but they are less likely to claim attention or authority in a supervision session and may remain invisible to the supervisor.

In group supervision, I invited supervisees to name some of the voices within the cluster of conversations that might be informing the work of their colleague, Jasmine. We were a diverse group of five clinical psychologists and systemic psychotherapists: a White British man, two White British women and two Black British women. I am a Black woman, born in South America and educated from primary school age in Britain. Between us we covered an age range from late twenties to mid-fifties and, using our profession as criteria, I would describe us as middle-class.

> Jasmine, a clinical psychologist, brought her client Anil to our regular monthly supervision session to explore her dilemma around 'ending work' with him and 'closing the case'. Anil, a man in his late thirties, was married with two children. He had come to the attention of the mental health service because of his 'self-harming behaviour'. Over time, his behavior had become progressively aggressive towards complete strangers, attracting the attention of the police service. We learned that Anil came to England from India as a young boy to join his parents, who had arrived some years earlier. His large extended family lived in close proximity and formed a close-knit community. We also learned that he had a disability that affected his speech.
>
> Jasmine had worked with Anil and his family for 18 months. She told us that initially he made good use of sessions with her, but recently he 'changed his mind' about seeing her and did not want his wife and family engaged in therapy sessions. Jasmine's team held a strong belief that

> Anil's behaviour was a response to the 'family dynamics', and that 'family work' would help make sense of his behaviour. Anil's parents, on the other hand, believed that medication was the best treatment for him and invited their local Member of Parliament (MP) to support their challenge of the professional system's treatment plans for their son.

Jasmine informed us that her community mental health team (CMHT) felt they had 'done all they could' for Anil and his family, had 'nothing more to offer' and her line manager told her to 'close the case'. Although the thought of closing the case brought 'a sense of relief' for Jasmine, she questioned whether she had 'done all I can' and wondered if she had 'failed the family'.

Making visible the voices within clusters of conversations

I was interested in the many different conversations about 'closing the case' that Jasmine was party to and wondered about other possible conversations unknown to her. Therefore, I invited the supervision group to name 'voices' of people they imagined might have an interest in whether or not the case should be closed. Among the voices identified were: Jasmine's line manager, colleagues, family, professional body, the GP, police, MP, Anil's mother, community, wife and children (illustrated in figure 4.1).

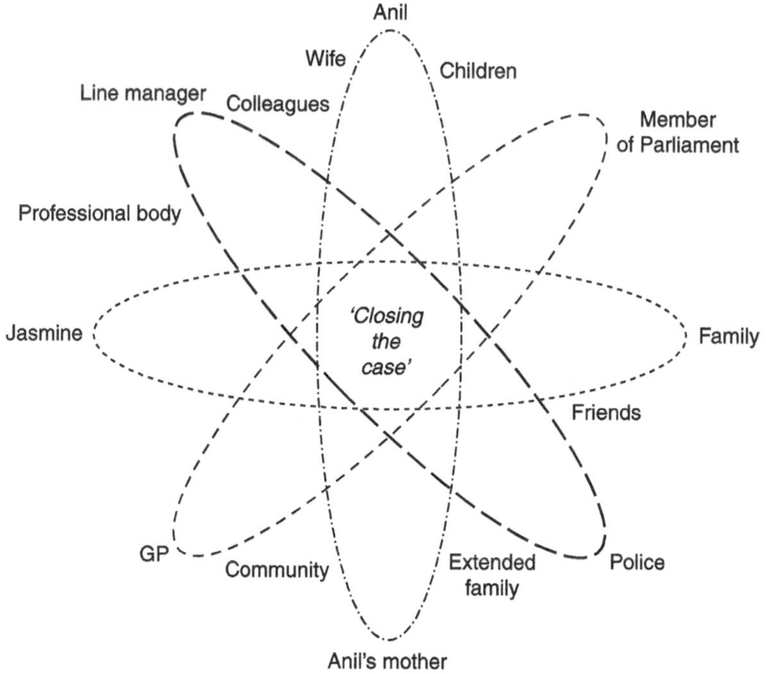

Figure 4.1 Making visible the voices in Jasmine's cluster of conversations

We went on to hypothesise (Palazzoli *et al.*, 1980) 'who was talking with whom about what?' in this cluster of conversations: which voices might be invisible to Jasmine and her team; which voices might command more or less entitlement for attention; and which voices were given more or less authority and legitimacy to speak and be heard. Identifying these voices sparked our curiosity about the multiverse of stories that might be told by Anil and his family and by Jasmine and her team.

For example, we hypothesised that the voice of Anil's community, invisible to Jasmine and her team, might attribute experiences that services were describing as 'mental health issues' to the work of evil spirits. These stories might bring shame and blame for Anil and his family, in turn constraining his inclination to take up the service on offer. The group also contemplated the voices and conversations invisible to Anil and his family that informed Jasmine as she coordinated his care: for instance, the voice of her line manager who needed to reconcile offering a service to distressed clients while managing the throughput of cases, and the voices of Jasmine's family who worried about the stress she was under.

Reflecting on how we embody positions in conversations

In conversations each person takes a position and offers or calls the other person into positions in a storyline (Harré and van Langenhove, 1999). Thus, we position ourselves and we are positioned by others. People will, therefore, have available to them certain positions, for example, wife, child, manager, therapist or supervisor, each associated with its cluster of rights, duties and responsibilities to act or not act in certain ways. The positions we take inform our perspectives and actions and have consequences for our relationships. (See Fredman, chapter 5 this volume, for further discussion of positioning.)

The positions available to us may be influenced by the identities we show in our bodies, for instance, our gender, age, "race" or physical abilities. Thus, in a society where being male, able-bodied, white and educated are highly valued and confer a range of privileges, the group considered how Anil might position Jasmine, as well as stories Jasmine might hold that could influence how she positioned Anil. For example, we hypothesised about some of the culturally-informed beliefs Anil might hold about women. We went on to think about how these might show in the descriptions given about his behaviour towards women and how they might invite him to position Jasmine as a White, educated, and professional young woman. Would it be significantly different to how he might position her had she been Asian or Black? We wondered about Jasmine's stories about non-White men and Asian men in particular. Which discourses on "race", gender, religion, might she be drawing on to inform how she positioned Anil? Was he to be feared or pitied or something else?

Embodying voices in the cluster of conversations

Sometimes I invite supervisees to embody the client's or a family member's voice in the supervision conversation. One way of doing this is to interview the 'internalised other', a method developed by Karl Tomm (1999) who posits that each of us internalises a community of voices that are part of our lived experiences and, if invited to, we can speak 'as if' we are that person. In supervision, I use *internalised other interviewing* to bring to life the perspective of a person or persons who are not present.

Interviewing the internalised other

I asked Jasmine if she would be interested in talking with me for a short time 'as if' she were her client, Anil. I invited her to use the pronoun 'I' as she responded in the 'voice' of Anil. I explained, 'I am not asking you to role-play, but rather to speak from your experience of Anil's [the other's] experience'. Thus, she would be free to speak of her own sense of what the client/other might say whether or not she had heard them actually express these thoughts. With Jasmine's agreement, I went on to interview her 'as if' she were Anil. Addressing her in the name of 'Anil', I asked Jasmine (embodying 'Anil'), a number of questions, such as, '"Anil", what were you hoping Jasmine could help you with?'; 'If your mother was here would she say the same or something different?' 'What happens, when you, "Anil", and your mother have different ideas; are you able to reach an agreement on your own or would you have to bring in other family members?'

The *internalised other interview* may last for 5–20 minutes. I then return to addressing the supervisee clearly in her own name, asking her again to speak in her own voice and to reflect on any new understandings or ideas that have emerged from the interview. After Jasmine had responded in the first person 'as if' Anil, I invited her colleagues in the supervision group, who had been quietly listening to the interview, to offer reflections (Andersen, 1987). Sharing their responses in a conversation between themselves while Jasmine listened, one colleague commented on the 'weariness' embodied in the voice of 'Anil' when Jasmine was describing Anil's mother's view that therapy was 'useless'. This resonated with Jasmine, who commented that, in discussions about the management of this case with her line manager, she often felt 'worn down' and lacking in energy.

We wondered whether Jasmine was experiencing ethical dilemmas that might explain her lack of energy. I suggested we use Domains of Action theory as a framework for making sense of Jasmine's thinking, feelings and action.

Reprising the Domains of Action

Domains of Action theory, as presented by Lang *et al.* (1990), invites us to think about ourselves as moral beings constantly travelling between domains as we manage our roles and responsibilities as health and social care practitioners in the agency contexts in which we work. Lang *et al.* identify *domains of production, explanation* and *aesthetics* in which practitioners may position themselves or be positioned.

The domain of production

The domain of production deals with universal truths, with policies and procedures, some of which may have their basis in legislation. In this domain there is right and wrong. Evidence is gathered and used to make judgements; and blame, with all the consequences that follow, can be apportioned. Working in the *domain of production* may show in our embodiment by, for example, how we direct our gaze away from the people we are talking to and towards our professional technologies like assessment forms or reports; how we sit, perhaps at or behind a desk; how we use our gestures or tone of voice to convey our professional authority or certainty.

I think of this as the '*what domain*'. '*What* is our contract for working?' '*What* are the rules of engagement?' '*What* are the anticipated outcomes?' '*What* should we do/*what* action is needed?' (for example, a judgement/recommendation/plan of action). In the *domain of production*, we considered: '*What* was Jasmine required to *do*?' '*What* was the intended outcome of her involvement?' '*What* were the responsibilities of others and how did these relate to Jasmine's distinct responsibilities?' 'To whom was Jasmine responsible?'

Jasmine told us that Anil was initially referred because of concern about his safety and the safety of the public. A multi-agency network was engaged to address concerns about risk, including: the police service (responsible for the public's safety); the referring GP, alongside the CMHT (responsible for Anil's mental health, well-being and, therefore, his personal safety) and the MP, invited by the family. Once Jasmine articulated her own responsibilities within the network as, 'formulating the concerns from a psychological perspective' and 'working with this formulation as far as Anil and the family agree', Jasmine came to a position of being able to say 'I have done what I needed to do to fulfil my contractual responsibilities to Anil and his family, my agency and the multi-agency systems'. Hence, we re-framed (Waltzawick *et al*., 1974) Jasmine's dilemma regarding closing the case as one of 'knowing when to disengage'.

Domain of explanation

In the *domain of explanation* we look at how meaning is made, rather than searching for the 'truth'. This does not mean that we give up ideas of what is right or wrong or condone illegal or immoral activities, but that we become *curious* about what a particular way of being and acting means in our lives and in the lives of the people with whom we are in conversation. In this domain we privilege 'curiosity' (Cecchin, 1987) in order to open space for many different truths to emerge. Therefore, we may listen more than we speak and our tone of voice may be softer. Our bodies may convey our curiosity as we find ourselves nodding or leaning towards the speaker, or show wonder or pain as our faces open or contract spontaneously in response to what we are hearing.

We enter *the domain of explanation* when we wish to explore alternatives so we can begin to understand the logic of how things are or have become. I think of this domain as the 'which' domain: *which* of these explanations or beliefs are more helpful? In the *domain of explanation* we explored the cluster of conversations Jasmine was part of; we wondered whether for Anil, an Indian man with limited education and a speech disability, Jasmine, a White professional, embodied all mental health and statutory services. To explore further some of the clusters of conversations we had identified in figure 4.1, we turned the spotlight on the voices of Anil's family, children and community. We generated hypotheses from the perspectives of "race", culture, religion and immigration. For example, we hypothesized how the family's religious beliefs might have informed their expectations about what should and could be done. We wondered about the stories told about marriage opportunities for Anil's children. We wondered, too, about which of the beliefs, expressed in Jasmine's conversations with Anil, might better fit with Eurocentric approaches to mental health and which might be more sympathetic to non-Eurocentric ways of thinking. In this way, we aimed to generate multiple perspectives that might open space for new ways for Jasmine to go on.

Domain of aesthetics

In the *domain of aesthetics*, we pay attention to how we do what we do. This is the domain in which we consider how we show respect for other people's feelings, beliefs and values, while managing our duties and responsibilities in the context of our agencies' policies and procedures. I think of this as the 'how' domain. '*How* will I do this?' 'What kinds of values and beliefs might influence my thinking about *how* I do what I do?' '*How* will I attend to my body and the bodies of those with whom I am meeting?' (e.g. '*How* could I arrange seating to best convey my intentions?' '*How* could I greet people or regulate my voice?').

In the *domain of aesthetics,* we reflected with Jasmine on *how* she could work collaboratively and respectfully with Anil and his family while holding safety as paramount at the centre of the assessment process. We also thought about *how* she might speak to Anil and his family about the possibility of ending work with her service.

Still struggling . . .

Jasmine appreciated the supervision group's validation of her experience, since they had 'echoed many conversations' she had had with herself, with colleagues, with Anil and with members of his family. However, she was still 'struggling with how I feel about continuing the work or closing the case'.

Up to this point we had been working in supervision within the *domains of production, explanation* and *aesthetics*. In the *domain of production*, Jasmine could justify the practical action of closing the case, yet she seemed to be 'struggling' with what Jim Wilson (2011) calls 'ethical dissonance', when we do something because it is practical, but it does not fit with our values. Boyd White (1984: 277) observes that:

> One is perpetually telling one's story to oneself and others, trying to shape things so that the next step fits with what has gone before, ceaselessly claiming significance for one's experience and actions and the question always is, in what language can or must one do these things?

Jasmine was 'still struggling'; perhaps because she did not have a way of giving an account of her action that fitted with her values. The unvoiced question we had not addressed was 'how do I (Jasmine) *give a coherent account* to myself and my audiences for the action (closing the case) I have been instructed to take?'

We often enter into the act of *giving account* to ourselves and others for our actions in an unself-conscious way. We know we have to make a judgement or decision, we may even be able to articulate our thinking, but the feelings and bodily sensations evoked by our judgements and decisions are usually part of an unspoken narrative. I propose that account-giving be located in a domain that is separate yet connected to the domains of *production, explanation* and *aesthetics* so that we might reflect with intention on what we are doing and how we are feeling about what we are doing. The name I have given this domain is '*rhetoric*'.

Introducing the domain of 'rhetoric'

The concept of rhetoric dates back to classical Greek philosophers Socrates, Isocrates, Plato and Aristotle. It has come to be viewed with cynicism and is often thought of as a means of manipulating or obscuring the truth. Aristotle, however, saw rhetoric as a system of persuasion based on knowledge and not manipulation or omission (Buzzell and Herzberg, 2000), a tool for practical debate and a means for persuading a general audience using probable knowledge to resolve practical everyday issues.

The way in which we, as human beings, *do* persuading is in conversation, using words as well as our bodies. When we step into the *domain of rhetoric*, we attend to what our words **do**. The *domain of rhetoric* can be defined as one in which we give account to ourselves and others for what we are doing. It is a place where we give a coherent story of our action in which our obligations and responsibilities are made transparent. In so doing we consider how we are making meaning in relationship with others, what identities we are calling into being for ourselves and our interlocutors, what relationships we are intending to foreground, what bodily sensations are evoked in these transactions and what beliefs and values they connect the speaker and listener to. Thus, this is a domain that privileges our ability to be self-reflexive.

I first began to give considered thought to the issue of *giving account* a number of years ago. There had been several 'serious case reviews' connected with child deaths in children's social care services. I was supervising a social worker who was expected to talk about her professional role in the child protection network following the death of a child. Two big concerns for her were 'telling the truth' and 'being believed'. She feared she might not have the language or words to make her intentions and actions clear to a panel that might be 'seeking to apportion blame'. She experienced this fear as 'paralysing'. She located the paralysis in her head and, more specifically, in her brain, as it affected her ability to think clearly. She had brought the issue to supervision in the hope that it might help release her from the sense of paralysis she was feeling.

A year or so later, I attended a workshop in which Barnett Pearce (2006) talked about the importance of how we give accounts to ourselves and other audiences that enable us to 'go on' in conversations in ways that are coherent with our beliefs, values and commitments about what we should and could do, our *moral logic.*[1] I thought back to that social worker and recognised that enabling her to *construct a coherent account* of events had required a way of enabling her explicitly to connect to her 'moral logic' (Pearce, 1994; 2007), in which her actions were embedded.

My work with the social worker had included helping her with naming and locating the bodily sensations (of fear and 'paralysis') that were part of the story of her moral logic. What she was experiencing in her body drew our attention to a dissonance between what she was being required to do (to defend and justify herself before the review panel) and what her sense of herself and her moral commitments required of her (to mourn the death of a child and to reflect on her own learning from this experience). She described how abhorrent it was to her to anticipate 'blame' for the death of a child as this was the antithesis of everything she stood for, as a woman and as a social worker committed to protecting children. The threatened discontinuity in her story of herself seemed to have led to her inability to *give an account*, and she experienced this in her body as a feeling of 'paralysis'.

As social beings, our identities and how we feel about these identities (that is our emotional connection to them) play a part in how we position ourselves and how others might position us in interpersonal communication. Stepping into the *domain of rhetoric* gives us permission to pause to ask the question: 'Who am I?' (in this moment, in this interaction) and 'How does who I am allow me to make sense of my roles and responsibilities?'

Continuing with the example of Jasmine, I want to show how I worked with the supervision group to invite them to position themselves in the *domain of rhetoric*.

Taking up a position in the domain of rhetoric

Working in the *domain of rhetoric,* I invited Jasmine to consider:

- Who is Jasmine (in this moment, in this interaction)? How does who she is allow her to make sense of her roles and responsibilities?
- What account does she need to give to herself in order to go on?

Who is Jasmine? Jasmine as a multi-being

Gergen (2008: 336) uses the term 'multi-beings' to illustrate that we are not one single, unified, independent person. He says that:

> The person is essentially constituted by a multiplicity of relationships. Some relations leave residues that are well practiced, while others leave little but whispers of possibility. The well-practiced residues are immediately to hand, such as the way one speaks to casual friends. Often we call these habits. They feel at the moment to be authentic, a reflection of the true self.

Thus, in asking 'who is Jasmine?', my invitation was to name some of the identities Jasmine wished to claim for herself and the identities the group offered her. In setting out to map Jasmine's identities my intention was to make as many of her perceived identities as possible visible, in order that she and we could explore the possible influence they might have on her thinking and acting.

Jasmine's peers in the supervision group called forth identities for her as 'thoughtful', 'responsible' and 'professional' in the way she approached her work with clients. Some identities she claimed for herself were as someone who was 'honest', 'sensitive', 'helpful', 'collaborative' and 'good at sharing information'. I wondered what identities she thought Anil might name for her if he was in the room with us. One of the group wondered whether he might say that Jasmine 'is a trier and doesn't give up easily'. I wondered who else might say that about Jasmine. Jasmine thought her parents might say she is 'determined'. This led me to ask whether those were aspects of herself that might be seen in her work context and by whom. Jasmine thought her manager might say that she is 'thorough' and that she 'pays attention to detail'. Another member of the group wondered what Jasmine thought Anil's mother might say. Without hesitation, Jasmine said: 'She would say I didn't understand anything and that I was only confusing Anil and putting wrong ideas in his head. I think she also sees me as having a lot of power.'

Listening to the body

Our words, and the stories we tell, cannot be divorced from the effects they have on our bodies and the bodies of those with whom we are in conversation (Bertrando and Gilli, 2008).

Curious about Jasmine's response to the question about Anil's mother's opinion, I asked what emotions that question and her response evoked for her. She said that it put her in touch with how 'powerless' she felt. It also made her feel 'sad', as she thought she was 'trying really hard' and 'doing [her] best to help', not just Anil but the whole family. I asked, 'If you were to name where those feelings – "sad", "powerless" – were located in your body, what would you say?' She thought for a while and said, 'My shoulders, definitely my shoulders and perhaps my stomach.' Jasmine went on to name the 'confusion and anxiety' she felt, connecting them to the 'knot' she felt in her stomach and the 'tightness' in her shoulders.

Our feelings often give us clues to what may be happening in the relationship and can offer a way to enter into conversation about discourses that are not easily articulated. Connecting with the 'confusion and anxiety' embodied in the 'tightness' in her shoulders and the 'knot' in her stomach, Jasmine described a strong story about the satisfaction she got from 'doing [her] best' which she recognised as part of a cluster of conversations about her identity as a daughter and as a student, overlapping with a cluster of conversations about achievement. She connected her current sense of 'powerlessness' and 'confusion' with the experience of doing her best in the work with Anil, but without the reward of feeling that she had succeeded in being helpful. Anil's family's challenge to the treatment plan and the recruitment of their MP confirmed her sense of failure.

I wondered whether Jasmine's sense of failure would be as great, greater or smaller if she had been working with a White British family. Jasmine thought that the fact that she was working across cultures added to her feeling of anxiety and the knot in her stomach was an indication that she was feeling out of her depth. Her biggest fear was of being accused of not making enough effort to understand this Asian family, using European values to determine the treatment offered Anil and judging him as non-compliant on that basis.

Giving account

Who are the audiences?

In response to my question, 'Who are the audiences to which you consider yourself accountable?' Jasmine thought that both the local MP and her professional body were particularly significant. We learned that another team in the agency was in the middle of a serious case review, following a death by suicide. The family at the centre of the inquiry was Asian and the questioning process had been experienced as hostile and blaming by her colleagues giving evidence to the inquiry. This was the context in which Jasmine found herself thinking about her line manager's recommendation for action.

In naming our audiences, we are also able to identify and explore our responsibilities and obligations and how we might discharge these in ways that are congruent with our personal and professional stories about ourselves in the context of our agencies. Jasmine chose to privilege her identity as an accountable clinician as she foregrounded the voices of the MP and the professional body to which she was affiliated. It seemed that this was informed by other conversations about the consequences for the agency and herself should circumstances result in Anil's situation becoming the focus of a serious case review. The 'struggle' Jasmine felt in relation to this case had led to her experiencing herself as indecisive, not being sure what to do or how she should *go on* (Cronen and Lang, 1994: 3).

Reflecting on Jasmine's struggle

In the conversation with Jasmine in the *domain of rhetoric*, a narrative began to emerge of how Jasmine's familiar and preferred identities might be at odds with the identities and actions ascribed to her by others. Her identity as 'professional', 'thoughtful', 'sensitive', for instance, was validated by the supervision group, but contradicted by Anil's mother who, Jasmine thought, saw her as 'not understanding anything' and 'putting wrong ideas' into Anil's head. Her preferred identity, as someone who 'doesn't give up easily', was at odds with her manager's instruction to close the case. Similarly, Jasmine's story of herself as 'doing my best' and 'achieving' was interrupted by the family's response to her work. All these stories of her identity were further shaken by Jasmine's own doubts about her ability to work across cultures.

Jasmine's 'struggle' was perhaps compounded by the different kinds of account required by different audiences. She identified the MP and her professional body as particularly significant audiences, foregrounding contexts in which she might be judged and held to account. But the kind of account she needed to give to these audiences, accounts of her adherence to protocol, procedure and evidence base, did not fully embrace the account she needed to give herself to satisfy her own moral commitments of helpfulness, sensitivity, collaboration and perseverance.

What account can Jasmine give to herself in order to go on?

In the midst of these contradictions and dissonances, Jasmine was struggling to give an account, to herself and others, either about her work or about closing the case. Knowing how to *go on* in this context, meant being able to act in ways congruent with her preferred identities and professional and personal values. I invited Jasmine's peers to participate in a *reflecting conversation* with each other in her presence, to share the ideas and questions that our conversation had generated. Finally I asked Jasmine, 'What is this conversation doing for you?' Jasmine reflected on some of the dissonances and the interruptions to her story of herself that had emerged in our conversation and in the group's reflections. What had struck her most powerfully was her realisation that she had been holding feelings she had been unable to speak, which had contributed to her inability to share her apprehension about closing the case with her manager. Doing so, she said, would have meant putting into words her uncertainty about working cross-culturally. This, she believed, would have challenged her own and her manager's story of her as a competent professional, since a significant proportion of her caseload involved families from the Indian sub-continent, Africa and Eastern Europe. Reconnecting with her preferred identities and naming her feelings of anxiety about doing or saying the wrong thing was, for Jasmine, a relief. It enabled her to release herself from positions and identities she felt she had been offered and had taken up – often with reluctance. It also enabled her to develop an account of her uncertainty in working cross-culturally that was coherent with her story of herself as an 'honest person' and 'ethical professional' who could identify gaps in her knowledge and bring her determination to the task of learning something new.

It is important to say that the aim in working with the ideas expressed here is not to reach a solution or a consensus. It is about helping practitioners to move towards the construction of new narratives that enable 'struggles' to dissolve and ways of going on to emerge. For Jasmine, the supervision conversations helped her to *go on* to have further conversations with her line manager to review the decision to close the case at that point. It also helped her to open up conversations about her training needs and how these could be met by her agency.

Conclusion

In our work we are constantly travelling between domains as we negotiate our actions and interactions in clusters of overlapping conversations. The Domains of Action theory provides a useful frame for punctuating and articulating this process, naming domains of *production*, *explanation* and *aesthetics*. In this chapter, I have intended to extend practitioners' thinking within the existing framework of Domains of Action theory by highlighting the activity of account giving, which I have argued should be located in a separate domain, which I have named *rhetoric*. The *domain of rhetoric* as I define it foregrounds our ability to be self-reflexive.

When supervisees speak of 'struggling' or not 'knowing how to go on', it may be that they have been unable to give an account of their actions that is coherent with their moral logic or story of who they are. In the *domain of rhetoric*, we explore the supervisee's identity stories, the audiences to their *account giving* and the ethical dissonances they may be experiencing. These dissonances, I have suggested, may first be experienced in the body, in physical sensation and emotion. Thus, by including the supervisee's embodied experience in the conversation, we can find that unexpected information can be released that helps the supervisee to connect to untold stories (Pearce, 2007) (see also Bownas, chapter 8). These processes can help to dissolve 'struggles', freeing the supervisee to give a coherent account of their actions and to know how to go on.

Following is a brief guide for supervisors who may wish to try working in the *domain of rhetoric* in supervision.

Guide 4.1 Guiding questions for the supervisor working in the domain of rhetoric

Naming identities

Who are *you* (supervisee) in this situation? What identities (abilities, characteristics) do you see in yourself? What might others involved in this situation say about you? Which of these identities most speak to your story of yourself, who you are and what you stand for? Are any of those identities at odds with these preferred stories of yourself?

Listening to the body

As you speak of these identities what emotions do you experience? Where in your body would you locate those feelings? What do these feelings and sensations connect you to? What might they draw our attention to that you have not yet spoken of?

Giving account

In this situation who are the audiences to whom you consider yourself accountable? What kind of *account (of your actions)* is needed for each audience? How do the accounts required by others fit with the account you need to give yourself to be consistent with your own story of who you are and what you stand for?

Reflecting and going on

If we reflect now on our conversation, might we notice any places where there is a disconnection with your familiar and preferred story of yourself? What account/s could you give that would satisfy your audiences and yourself? What would such an account enable you to do?

Note

1 In this chapter I think of 'morality' as related to issues of honour, dignity and character. A 'moral order' is the set of practices we agree on as a group of persons for the promotion of the morality of that group. The different roles and identities we assume in our lives (e.g. parent, lover, therapist or citizen) have different moral orders, different sets of rights, duties and obligations. 'Moral logic' refers to how our actions are connected to the moral order of our identity or role in a particular moment of interaction: those things we *must* do within our moral order. Imagine, for instance, that I am in a room with a woman who is crying in distress. In that moment if my identity is that of close friend I may feel I *must* go to her, hold and comfort her. But if my identity is that of therapist, depending on the moral order of my community of therapists, I may feel I *must not* embrace or comfort her, that I *must* allow her tears and help her to give words to them (Pearce, 1994).

References

Andersen, T. (1987) The reflecting team: dialogue in clinical work. *Family Process*, 26, 415–28.

Bertrando, P. and Gilli, G. (2008) Emotional dances: therapeutic dialogues as embodied systems. *Journal of Family Therapy*, 30, 362–73.

Buzzell, P. and Herzberg, B. (2000) *The Rhetorical Tradition: Reading from Classic Times to the Present*. New York: Bedford/St Martins.

Boyd White, J. (1984) *When Words Lose Their Meaning*. Chicago: University of Chicago.

Cecchin, G. (1987) Hypothesizing, circularity and neutrality revisited: an invitation to curiosity. *Family Process*, 26, 405–13.

Cronen, V. and Lang, P. (1994) Language and action: Wittgenstein and Dewey in the practice of therapy and consultation. *Human Systems: The Journal of Systemic Consultation and Management*, 5, 5–34.

Gergen, K. J. (2008) Therapeutic challenges of multi-being. *Journal of Family Therapy*, 30, 335–50.

Harré, R. and van Langenhove (eds) (1999) *Positioning Theory*. Oxford: Blackwell.

Lang, P., Little, M. and Cronen, V. (1990) The systemic professionals: Domains of Action and the question of neutrality. *Human Systems: The Journal of Systemic Consultation and Management*, 1, 34–40.

The Oxford Popular English Dictionary (1990) (Revised ed. 1995). Oxford: Parragon Book Services & Magpie Book Services.

Palazzoli Selvini, M., Boscolo, L., Cecchin, G. and Prata, G. (1980) Hypothesizing, circularity, neutrality: three guidelines for the conductor of the session. *Family Process*, 19, 2–12.

Pearce, W. B. (1994) *Interpersonal Communication: Making Social Worlds*. New York: HarperCollins.

Pearce, W. B. (1995) Research and evaluation: a systemic approach. KCC International Workshop, 3–7 July, London.

Pearce, W. B. (2006) *Designing Meetings that Facilitate Dialogic Communication.* KCC Workshop, 2–3 October, London.

Pearce, W. B. (2007) *Making Social Worlds: A Communication Perspective*. Oxford: Blackwell Publishing.

Postman, N. (1985) *Amusing Ourselves to Death: Public Discourse in the Age of Show Business.* New York: Penguin.

Tomm, K. (1999) Co-constructing responsibility. In S. McNamee, K. J. Gergen and Associates. *Relational Responsibility: Resources for Sustainable Dialogue*. Thousand Oaks, CA: Sage.

Watzlawick, P., Weakland, J. H. and Fisch, R. (1974) *Change: Principles of Problem Formation and Problem Resolution.* New York, London: W. W. Norton & Co.

Wilson, J. (2011) *Child Focussed Practice*. Presentation, Institute of Family Therapy, 11 January, London.

5 Using supervision to prepare our bodies for the therapeutic relationship

Glenda Fredman

I work within public health services for children, older people and adults affected by intellectual disabilities where I meet with people in individual therapy, family therapy and in large networks with other practitioners. I also participate in meetings with managers to address organisational strategy and service planning. We carry feelings into all these sorts of encounters and our feelings can influence our presence and connection with the people with whom we engage. For example, Chris (below) recognises that 'irritation' interrupted his listening and thinking, interfering in his relationship with his client (Ms Jennings) and, later in the chapter, Rina describes how a feeling of 'dread' stopped her from engaging with the mother of a client.

In this chapter I describe a supervision practice, *preparing our emotional postures*, which invites practitioners to *prepare our bodies* and *our selves* before meeting with clients, colleagues and professionals. The approach is intended to enable us to transform unwanted feelings (like irritation, frustration or dread) and unwanted emotional postures (like defending, controlling or blaming) towards preferred positions, which are more likely to invite relationships of respect, safety and collaboration that involve mutual listening and appreciation.

> In a supervision session, Chris, a White male psychologist in his early thirties, asked for help with 'managing the attitude' of Ms Jennings, the mother of a nine-year-old boy, who had been referred to his service for help with 'anxiety'. Chris complained that she was 'always on [the boy's] case'; Chris found her 'whiny voice so irritating' that he was finding it 'hard to listen to her'.

As practitioners and supervisors committed to the well-being of the people with whom we work, such as Chris, we often have strong feelings about a person or a situation, which affects the sort of relationship we might create with people. I have developed this supervision practice to address both practitioners' and clients' contributions to the therapeutic relationship. This approach takes into consideration not only how the client might meet and receive the practitioner, but also what practitioners might be feeling and how *they* are entering the encounter.

Language is saying and doing, speaking and acting

> Chris was bringing his unwanted feeling of 'irritation' to supervision. He had the idea that he could 'manage the attitude' of Ms Jennings, and of himself, by 'expressing' the irritation 'to get it all out' (his words) and then go on to be with Ms Jennings without irritation. When I asked him, 'What effect does expressing the irritation in this way have on your body?' he laughed ironically that, 'I think I'm becoming irritating too now. It's like she's rubbing off on me . . .'

Language involves both saying and doing. Movement always accompanies our expressions of words, both those outer movements more visible to the audience and the subtler, personal movements, evident only to the speaker. Cronen and Pearce (1985) have coined the term 'speech-acts' (originally from Austin, 1965) to reflect both the speaking and the acting involved in communication. Thus, body movements accompany the words we utter as living activity, embodied utterances or expressions (Shotter, 1993). Chris's response, 'I'm becoming irritating . . . she's rubbing off on me' suggests that he was 'doing' the 'irritation' both with words and with his body.

Words are not only heard or received, but they also move the talker. These movements can be seen and felt by the listener who, in turn, is moved: we touch each other and our selves with our expressions, and the words we speak move both our selves and others to different positions. Thus, as we speak, our expressions shape our bodies and as we go on expressing and responding to each other's expressions, we continually shape and reform our relationships. Therefore language is formative, in that it constitutes our bodies and creates our relationships. Hence, saying what we feel about clients does not simply ventilate the feeling or get it out of our system; rather our expressions constitute our bodies. With our words/actions, our speech-acts, we form and 'in-form' our selves and each other. Simply expressing the unwanted 'irritation' about Ms Jennings in supervision, therefore, did not help rid Chris of the feeling. Rather it seemed to position him to re-experience those unwanted feelings so that he recreated and embodied the irritation, with the risk of taking the 'irritation' back into his session with the client.

Therefore, we have to do more with our feelings than simply express or 'ventilate' them. In this chapter, I offer a supervision practice for transforming these feelings (Fredman, 2004) through different kinds of talk that invite us to change our bodies and reposition our selves. In supervision and pre-session preparations for meetings[1] with people, therefore, I pay particular attention to the words we use when talking about people. Mindful that we embody our utterances, that our ways of talking shape and position our bodies, I invite attention, in supervision, to how our talking positions us bodily to enter the session.

Emotional postures

Our encounters begin with bodily expression; from the start we meet each other in and with our bodies. Therefore it is our embodied practices that are primary, 'not the word, but our spontaneous responsiveness' to each other and the circumstances of our situation (Shotter, 2006: 10). Griffith and Elliot Griffith (1994: 66) describe how we meet each other in 'emotional postures' that involve our bodies' readiness to respond and that focus our attention towards others and ourselves in different ways. Our bodies are poised for acting and responding. We experience and show these postures bodily, and we notice and are affected by the postures of the other. In emotional postures of 'tranquillity' the body is relaxed and our attention is focused towards ourselves, as in daydreaming or musing, or towards connecting with another person, as in wondering, reflecting, listening or creating. In emotional postures of 'mobilisation', on the other hand, the body is physically poised for action; vigilant for threat and ready to defend or attack. Attention is focused outward and our bodies are primed to predict or control the other as in investigating, justifying, scorning, shaming, controlling, distancing, protesting and defending.

The emotional postures we engage in influence the quality of conversation we can have with each other. In a posture of 'tranquillity', therefore, we are able to enjoy the mutual touching of each other with words, voices, eyes or hands. Touching with words or bodies in a relationship marked by 'mobilisation', however, might be experienced as threatening or entrapping. Therefore, I offer this supervision practice as a sort of pre-session ritual for practitioners to prepare their bodies and their selves to enter meetings. Reflecting on the postures we might meet or carry into our meetings with people is one way we can prepare ourselves to position our bodies to invite curiosity, mutual listening and respect; where touching each other with words and actions is mutually enjoyable and attention is focused on connecting with each other and on reflecting and musing.

Preparing our emotional postures: a pre-session ritual

In the following example, I describe how Rina and I used supervision to prepare her *self* for an anticipated telephone conversation with Erica Vaughan that 'filled [Rina] with dread'.

> Rina, the manager of Magnolia Lodge, a residential home for young adults affected by intellectual disabilities, asked in a monthly group supervision for help with 'what to say' to Erica Vaughan, the mother of Tommy, a young man identified as 'autistic with moderate learning disabilities'. Rina explained that she 'had to phone Mrs Vaughan' who was 'not satisfied with Magnolia Lodge's care' of her son; Mrs Vaughan had 'always been difficult' and recently had 'started complaining again about Tommy's care . . . that his clothes were not ironed . . . his hair was not washed'. We learned that over the past year Erica Vaughan had developed a close supportive relationship with Tommy's keyworker, Avril, whom she described as 'always going the extra mile and a half for Tommy'. Avril had recently left her post. Mrs Vaughan did not like

the new young, male key worker who, she complained, did 'not understand Tommy'. She had started visiting the home daily and complained that the 'staff send me away with a flea in my ear'. Rina had written to Mrs Vaughan to 'explain about Magnolia Lodge's visiting policy – we only ask her to let staff know when she is coming'. Mrs Vaughan had responded with 'an abusive phone call to the administrator . . . demanding that Tommy be allocated another key worker . . . someone older, with experience of life, and a woman'. Rina was 'dreading making this call so much' that she had 'put it off five times – I have to do it today!'

Contemplating the emotional postures of clients

To enable Rina to prepare herself for the telephone conversation with Erica Vaughan, I invited her to anticipate what postures, responses and expressions she might encounter when Erica answered the phone. For example, did she think Erica wanted this phone call? What might she be expecting from Rina? How might Erica express how she was feeling? What might Erica want Rina to appreciate about her?

GLENDA: Do you think Mrs Vaughan wants this call?

RINA: Oh yes – she keeps trying to get hold of me.

GLENDA: How is she likely to be feeling when you call her?

RINA: I am sure she will be in a state.

GLENDA: What sort of state?

RINA: (Talking quickly) **Livid** because Avril is not available. She'd much rather be talking to **her**. **Fuming** about the letter I wrote her . . . she **screamed** at the secretary who was nice to her. She sees me as a totally **evil** person . . . She'll probably want to **tear a strip off me.**

GLENDA: What do you think Mrs Vaughan will want you to appreciate about her?

RINA: (Pausing and then slowing her speech) Er . . . that she is a mother committed to her son . . . that she is a good mother . . . Avril gave her a lot of time boosting her self-esteem . . .

GLENDA: What else might she want you to appreciate about her – her situation?

RINA: That she has rights too. She doesn't want to be fobbed off . . . She is tired of – she wants someone to help her.

In this way we began to consider whether Mrs Vaughan was likely to be relaxed and open to reflecting and connecting or tense and poised for action, for example watching out for criticism, rejection or blame, and so primed to defend or even put the phone down. We considered whether her attention would be focused inwards on listening and reflecting or outwards on, for example, justifying, distancing or defending.

Contemplating the emotional posture of clients in this way can open space for a 'feelingful way of seeing' (Bakhtin, 1981: 186). I noticed that each time Rina expressed specific words (in **bold** above) her body tensed and she spoke in a loud voice with pressure of speech. As she took Mrs Vaughan's position in response to my question '*What do you think she wants you to appreciate about her?*' Rina's speech slowed and softened and the volume of her voice slightly muted.

Contemplating the emotional posture of the supervisee/practitioner

I went on to explore with Rina her expectations and apprehensions of the forthcoming conversation with Mrs Vaughan. Inviting her to tune in to how she might feel and what she might show through her body, I asked her to anticipate the possible postures she might carry into their forthcoming conversation, with the intention that these questions might invite her to reflect relationally (Burnham, 2005) on how her posture might affect not only how she could be with Mrs Vaughan, but also what kinds of atmosphere and relationship she could or could not create with her.

GLENDA: So when you start dialing – what will be going on with your body?

RINA: I'll have a sore back – I hold all my tension in my back – it is always sore when I am stressed . . . (lifting her shoulders) my shoulders will be in my ears . . .

GLENDA: How will your body show what you are feeling?

RINA: I will be looking at the phone in dread and hoping no one comes in the room and sees me.

GLENDA: What would others notice about you – if they saw you?

RINA: (Slowing her speech and speaking more softly) I think it would be more my tone . . .

GLENDA: Your tone – what will it be like? Can you show me?

RINA: (Laughing self-consciously) Uhm – I don't know if I can do it. (Breathing in) I would be all polite (said with a staccato voice). It won't be relaxed or friendly . . . it will be highly-professional and rather stilted. I won't be sure whether to call her Erica or Mrs Vaughan. I called her Mrs Vaughan last time and she said I was insulting her.

GLENDA: And was it the words 'Mrs Vaughan' she experienced as insulting? Or was it 'more the tone' as you put it? Would she notice anything in your tone?

RINA: I'm sure she'd pick it up – a sort of clippedness – she may feel I am a bit terse.

Considering preferred postures

I also invited Rina to consider whether these were her preferred postures and to contemplate the postures she might wish to create.

GLENDA: How would you prefer your tone to be with Erica?

RINA: Flowing . . . not stilted . . . I would just talk instead of artificial – not falsely friendly or standoffish like some sort of bureaucrat in customer relations trying to avoid saying anything.

We went on to reflect on the effect of tone and posture on the therapeutic relationship with questions like: 'How might that tone affect your conversation with Erica?' 'How might your tone and your body posture affect the positions you can or cannot take in the conversation?' 'If you adopted a different posture/tone, what might you do/how might that be?' In this way we addressed how we might invite an atmosphere of respect, safety and collaboration.

GLENDA: What sort of atmosphere do you want to create with Erica? What sort of relationship?

RINA: A respectful one – we don't need to love each other – but for us to feel we can work with her – for her to feel – I suppose for her to trust us that we are trying our best.

GLENDA: So what tone is likely to invite . . .

RINA: Certainly not ultra-polite . . . Uh . . . talking less maybe . . . sitting and listening. Approaching it as if I really do like her and not in a way terrified she is going to snap and yell – being frightened she will snap is paralysing. If I did not feel that, then I could be more interested in her – ask her questions. There needs to be safety too.

GLENDA: So what would you be doing with your body to invite an atmosphere of respect?

RINA: Assuring her of my best intentions.

GLENDA: How do you do that?

RINA: Just listening to what she has got to say . . . (Laughs) I could do an impersonation of Harlene Andersen. How does she do it? (Slightly caricaturing, she cocks her head to one side and nods slowly.)

GLENDA: That sort of listening – what could that make possible?

RINA: I think I would be less defensive because I am focusing on **her** – not my fear.

GLENDA: To invite an atmosphere of safety . . . what could you do with your body, your voice?

RINA: (Laughs) Her safety or mine? . . . Safety is about not being attacked . . . So making statements like 'It's been decided' – the power thing makes her feel attacked. Practising how to word things like 'We'd really like to help', and make her feel less attacked. I don't feel unsafe – I just feel my professional identity is battered. It is really difficult to feel I have done such a bad job. The staff here have always thought I was really good at talking with difficult mothers. But it is different on the phone – you need to slow down – maybe say 'Let's check – have I got this right' . . .

GLENDA: What tone would you use when you are checking back like that?

RINA: I'd need to be careful I am not patronising – telephones can be so difficult – I could try to speak slower than her speed – concentrate on slowing down instead of matching her – it's a bit like dancing to the same tune.

GLENDA: Dancing to the same tune – can you say some more? How would you prefer to be with her – to dance with her?

RINA: Er . . . being in step? Not fighting. As a mother she has spent her entire life fighting people for Tommy. This must have felt like a lifelong battle. I would like her to be able to trust me like Avril – someone she can feel safe with. One of the people she can turn to.

As Rina spoke of her preferred tone, her voice softened and her pace slowed. Her awareness that it was 'more my tone . . . the clippedness' that Erica Vaughan was likely to 'pick up' shows how the meaning of what we say lies not simply in the form or pattern of the words we use, but in the way we express them, 'in our intoning' (Shotter, 2008: 508).

Intoning of voice

Our words intertwine with our bodily expression, including the quality of voice, pitch, tenor, timbre, pacing, so that the 'movement' of our words can express more than the words themselves. When Chris complained of Ms Jennings' 'whiny voice', he could not recall her words, at all.

I had always experienced Chris as a thoughtful mild-mannered man with a soft gentle voice. When he spoke of his 'irritation' with Ms Jennings, I noticed that his body appeared to stiffen and the pitch of his voice went up an octave or two. I was aware of my throat constricting and my inclination to turn away or stop him talking to avoid what I was experiencing as the piercing of his high-pitched voice.

Bakhtin (1981) describes how we 'populate' our words with our intentions, feeling and evaluation, adapting our talk to the meanings we want to get across. We exert effort to make our talk communicate what we are trying to express and this effort comes across in the 'emotional-volitional tone' (Bakhtin, 1993: 32) of the speaker.

However, we cannot always anticipate the effects of our spontaneous reactions. When Chris remarked on Ms Jennings's 'whiny' voice, not only did he express his feeling of 'irritation', he also inhabited the phrase with his own tone, which came across to me as critical and blaming. Not only did I find it hard to listen to Chris, I also found I could not speak, anticipating that I too would speak in the sort of 'irritating whiny' voice he disparaged.

I really like Bakhtin's (1981: 293) use of the phrase 'populate our words' since 'populate' holds connotations of 'people', 'inhabit' and also 'colonise', and for me reflects how our tone, which includes our accent, is intricately woven with our identity. There have been times in my life when people have commented negatively on the quality of my voice, in particular my Southern African accent. For example, as a trainee I felt wounded when a supervisor asked me, 'How do you think the Black nursery staff will feel about working with you when they hear your South African accent?' (At that time anyone or anything South African was strongly associated with racism. I did not identify myself as 'South African'; having come from Zimbabwe.). Since I have experienced negative attributions to my voice, like this one, as painfully undermining of my preferred identity or as a sort of colonisation, I wanted to take care how I responded to Chris, both his spontaneous reaction to Ms Jennings' voice and my spontaneous reaction to his reactions and to his voice.

We are never speaking neutrally without interest and our tone expresses how, as speakers, we expect another to respond to our words. Therefore, starting from the position that Chris's tone embodies something of his expectation or anticipation of a response or perhaps even an answer from me, I asked 'What would you like to get from our conversation? How would you like me to respond to what you have shared with me so far today?' Chris's wish 'to feel less irritated' and 'more empathic' with Ms Jennings opened space for us to explore 'How does Ms Jennings' voice make you feel? Are you experiencing that feeling here now? What do you want me to appreciate about that feeling? What do you want to happen? Why is that important to you?' As Chris engaged with his own commitment to 'feel more compassion' so he could 'listen, reflect' and 'work more creatively' with Ms Jennings, the pitch of his voice lowered and the pace of his talk slowed. In turn, my throat relaxed and I was able to change my posture, leaning towards Chris, focusing on him with my eyes and softening my tone. Together we were able to go on to consider what Ms Jennings might be wanting from their work together.

According to Vygotsky (1986) and Bakhtin (1993), everything we express and experience is intonated; our tone carries our intention, feeling and evaluative attitude, what matters to us and how important it is. Therefore, starting from the position that Ms Jennings' 'whiny' intonation was an expression of *her* feeling, intention and evaluation of her situation, I invited Chris to consider: 'What might Ms Jennings' voice be feeling/trying to express? What is it trying to communicate about what is important to her? What does she want you to appreciate about what she is feeling/what is important to her/what she wants to happen? How much do you think that matters to her?'

Within this supervision session, Chris began to wonder whether Ms Jennings 'feels I am not listening to her'; 'maybe she wants me to appreciate that she is really worried and feels I am not taking her seriously?' At our next supervision, Chris told me that our conversation had helped him engage with Ms Jennings 'to the point that she said to me, "You are really different today – you seem more relaxed"'.

Positioning

There are times when we find it difficult, challenging or even unacceptable to modify or moderate our bodily postures when anticipating meeting another. Often this difficulty presents when our emotional postures are intricately connected to our positions in a storyline that involves our moral order, identity and power relationships. For example, I noticed that each time Rina used the phrase 'difficult mother/s' these words seemed to pull her towards an unwanted posture she described as 'standoffish', or 'patronising'. Not only did the words shape her body and voice, but also seemed to be positioning her to 'manage' Erica.

In situations like this, I draw on Rom Harré's positioning theory (Davies and Harré, 1990; Harré and van Langenhove, 1999) to further inform preparing for the therapeutic relationship with supervisees. According to Harré, when we relate with each other we position each other in a story. Each person takes up positions and invites or calls the other person into positions in a storyline. The storyline may or may not be shared by the persons interacting with each other. Position calls are initially non-verbal and positioning relates to the moment. People can be positioned by others or position themselves, for example as powerful or powerless, dominant or submissive, confident or apologetic, definitive or tentative, authorised or unauthorised. In supervision therefore, we can consider the respective storylines of practitioners and clients, which involves reflecting with supervisees on the positions they may be invited into by others present and considering the positions they are likely to call others into.

Contemplating positioning and storylines of clients

Drawing on Harré's positioning theory, I explored whether Rina thought Erica shared and preferred this 'difficult mother to-be-managed' position and how Rina thought Erica positioned *her* in her preferred storyline.

GLENDA: What do you think Erica's story is about? What is happening between you and her?

RINA: Er. I'm not sure . . . I think she believes that because of resources we are not prepared to offer her son what he needs – we are not listening to her – we don't care about Tommy like she does.

GLENDA: Where does she get that from?

RINA: We had a difficult time with her in the past – before Avril became Tommy's keyworker. I know she felt Avril really got Tommy and, being older, they had the same view of life. I don't know what happened between her and Luke [new key worker].

GLENDA: What position is she giving you in this story?

RINA: (Sighing) Bureaucratic service manager.

The different services in which we work are informed by different worldviews, grand narratives or discourses (Burr, 2003). These different discourses offer people different positions in relation to each other. For example in hospitals, the medical discourse positions nurses, doctors and physiotherapists as 'professionals' and people using the service as 'patients'; our systemic team positions service users as 'clients' or 'young people' and 'families' and ourselves as 'practitioners' or 'therapists'. Within the Magnolia Lodge service, Rina was positioned as 'manager', service users like Tommy as 'residents' and staff as (key-, social- or support-) 'workers'; Erica was positioned as 'Tommy's mother'. I began to wonder whether Rina was *choosing* to call Erica into the position of 'difficult mother' and how Rina preferred to position herself in this storyline.

Contemplating positioning and storylines of the practitioner

I, therefore, went on to invite Rina to reflect on the position from which she was working with Erica, exploring her storyline and the positions she preferred to offer.

GLENDA: What position do you prefer to take with Erica? Who do you want to be with her?

RINA: I can't do anything about being the manager – that's my job. But I'd prefer to be a colleague of Avril – someone who supported Avril.

GLENDA: Supported Avril in what – what was Avril's story of Erica?

RINA: She felt huge compassion for Erica. They came from the same background and she didn't see Avril as an authority figure.

Each discourse involves its own moral order, prescribing and proscribing rights and responsibilities for how people should and should not act in certain contexts, so that positions also signal something about power relationships. In the early stages of interactions we construct our view of the other out of our knowledge of our familiar discourses. The discourses out of which we act position us, both practitioners and clients, within the therapeutic relationship. Each position brings with it a variety of expectations, explanations and interpretations about how the person relates to others. Having taken up a particular position, the person sees the world from that position and how we take up positions has consequences for the way we respond and for the way we experience our relationships. Rina could 'not do anything about being [in the position of] manager' and accepted her responsibility to manage the service. However, she preferred Erica to relate to her as 'a colleague of Avril' who 'supported her [with] huge compassion', rather than an 'authority figure' or the 'bureaucratic' voice of the service.

We embody the cultures and discourses of our gender, age, health, ethnicity, race, class, sexuality and professions; they shape our physical appearance, our voice (accent, inflection and intonation), our postures and our dress. How we embody our cultures opens or closes positions we can take and offer others through our bodies. We can use supervision to reflect on the range of possible positions we are likely to be offered and perceived to take up through our embodiment of our cultures and personal and professional discourses. We can go on to consider how different positions might inform, enable or constrain the rights of people involved to speak, contribute and act. For example, I asked Rina, 'How might the similarities and difference between you in age and status be influencing how Erica feels towards you/what she expects from you?', and 'Do you think your difference in race and that you are both women is enabling or constraining how you work together?'

> Rina noted that Erica and Avril 'come from the same background'. (Both were White, working-class women in their late fifties who had raised their families as sole parents.) She thought this 'immediately gave Avril the heads-up . . . to connect with Erica' who felt 'safe with the familiarity'.

As a professionally qualified, younger, British-born, Asian woman in a management position, Rina was aware she could 'not do anything about being a manager'. Neither could she embody Avril's age, ethnicity or class. However, she could use supervision to explore how her posture and voice opened or closed space for different positions and how different positions she took could enable or constrain her tone and voice. Thus, we can use supervision to enable practitioners to extend their repertoire of positions and emotional postures, by inviting them to generate and name alternate positions with the following sorts of questions: 'If you adopted a different posture/tone, what might you do?' 'How might you be?' 'What other positions might you take/invite?' 'What other story could you tell of what is happening here/who you are?' 'How could you create opportunities for taking alternative positions?' 'Do you think [client] will accept the position you offer?' 'What positions do you prefer to create?' 'How might your posture affect the positions you can/cannot take?'

> Thus, I went on to explore positioning with Rina, asking, 'How might your voice tone affect who you can be with Erica? Uh – like – does the "clippedness" you mentioned make it easier to be more like Avril's compassionate colleague or more of an authority figure?' Rina was clear that

> she wanted to 'show I am thoughtful . . . interested' and believed that her 'super-polite voice' was likely to create even more of a distance between her and Erica. She said she would 'have to live with knowing that Erica will not be happy with what we can offer Tommy . . . but I can listen and appreciate that and not get in a row'.

As she spoke, Rina recognised that entering the conversation with a 'super-polite voice' was more likely to position her as an authority figure and could interfere with creating a useful collaborative dialogue with Erica. She began to generate different positions from which to talk with Erica including 'colleague who supported Avril' and 'listener' and adopted different postures like 'compassion' and 'appreciation'.

Contemplating our own positioning involves taking a reflexive position on our own storylines including our personal and professional moral orders. When we start to talk about a position we move into a reflexive position and this makes our positioning more intentional implying we have a choice (Burnham, 2012). In this way, we might learn to 'master' (Vygotsky, 1986) our spontaneous reactions by deliberately giving ourselves appropriate verbal instructions at significant moments (Shotter, 2006).

In group supervision, I usually invite the group to offer contributions that might help the supervisee become reflexive to their own positions, positioning and storylines, thereby exploring further alternative positions that could open space for their preferred relationship with the client (Fredman, 2007). I have adapted Tom Andersen's *reflecting team* method (Andersen, 1991), whereby group members reflect in the presence of the therapist to invite the therapist into preferred emotional postures. The supervision group members have a conversation with each other in front of the supervisee, while the supervisee is invited to listen. Group members usually begin by reflecting on their understanding of the supervisee's experience of the dilemma and the help the supervisee is requesting. We have an agreement that the supervisee can stop the reflections when they have heard enough or if the conversation is proving unhelpful. For example, I have asked *my* peer supervision group to stop reflecting when they have joined my unwanted negative connotation of people. I have redirected them to find more helpful frames or connotations when their talks have invited postures antagonistic to those I preferred.

> By the end of the supervision conversation and having heard contributions from the supervision group, Rina shifted to a markedly different position in relation to the anticipated phone call. She moved from a story of Erica Vaughan as a 'difficult mother' to the dilemma that 'I cannot change Tommy's keyworker – so that is not good news for her. But as head of service I have to make that call – that is my responsibility, it is part of my job – but I do have good intentions – I can try and listen and appreciate Erica's dissatisfaction – I don't have to justify –

I can listen and apologise and avoid a sulky tone. That might keep it calm. She might be aggravated – I don't have to be – I can just feel I have done my best.'

Preparing our bodies for the therapeutic relationship

In this chapter, I have identified different parts of an approach to preparing our selves for the therapeutic relationship in supervision. These include: anticipating the clients' emotional postures that the practitioner/supervisee might meet; contemplating the emotional posture the practitioner/supervisee might carry into the meeting; considering which postures are preferred to approach the other and how different postures might affect the therapeutic relationship. We can also invite supervisees to contemplate how their gender, age, health, ethnicity, race, class, sexuality and profession shape their physical appearance, postures and voice; what others might notice and attribute to their own expressions and postures; and the possible effects on their relationship with the people they meet. In chapter 3, Philip Messent names the need for himself, as a supervisor in a 'position of power and influence', to examine the part his whiteness, age and class play in interactions with supervisees of different cultures. He offers supervisors questions to invite mutual exploration with supervisees of their embodied cultural difference and to invite reflection on how they are likely to be received by others from different cultures. Nick Pendry (chapter 2) offers exercises for supervisors to invite reflection on racial identity and track the impact of "race" on personal and professional lives with supervisees in supervision and training. We can also engage supervisees in anticipating the positions they and clients offer each other, contemplating their preferred positions within their respective storylines before generating a repertoire of alternative positions and postures with supervisees.

In group supervision, members of the group can use questions from the practice guide provided at the end of this chapter to interview the practitioner/supervisee requesting help. Reflections from the supervision group can further invite supervisees to become reflexive to their posture and positioning with respect to the therapeutic relationship. Practitioners can use this approach in *self-supervision* by allowing time before the session to ask themselves some of the *emotional preparing* questions in the guide at the end of this chapter. Or they can invite a supervisor or another colleague to ask them these questions. We have been surprised to find that a colleague's questioning and listening to our responses can help us not only become mindful of how we are being received, but also engage us with our preferred postures, even when the colleague has no idea about the content or context of our proposed meeting. Rarely do we use, or indeed need, the entire range of practices described above. We have found the questions marked in **bold** with an asterisk* in the practice guide most useful.

Guide 5.1 Preparing our selves for the therapeutic relationship

Contemplating emotional postures of clients

- **What postures might practitioner/supervisee meet?**
  - **How are they (clients) likely to feel on arriving to meet you?***
  - Do (clients) want this meeting? What might they be expecting?
  - **How might the social (e.g. gender, class, ethnicity) difference/similarity between you influence their feelings/expectations?***
  - How might they show/express how they are feeling?
  - **What might they want you to appreciate about them?***

Contemplating practitioner/supervisee emotional postures

- **With what postures might the practitioner enter the meeting?**
  - Are you (practitioner) looking forward to this meeting?
  - What feelings will you be taking into this meeting? Will you be carrying anything over from the last meeting?
  - When you first meet with (clients), what might you notice in their bodies or experience in your own body?
  - How might you respond to the person?
  - **How might your body/voice/tone show what <u>you</u> are feeling?***
  - **What will the others notice (about you)/hear in your voice?***
  - **How might the (age, gender, ethnicity etc.) social difference/similarity between you influence what they notice?***

Considering preferred postures

- **Which postures invite preferred atmosphere?**
  - Is this how you prefer to feel/be with these people?
  - What sort of atmosphere do you want to create? What sort of relationship (e.g. respect, safety and collaboration)?
  - How might that posture/ tone affect how you can be with the people in the room?
  - How might that posture affect the positions you can or cannot take in the session with these people?
  - **Which posture/tone is more likely to invite the atmosphere you want to create?***
  - **How would you prefer to be with this person? What do you want your body/voice to show?***

- **Contemplating positioning and storylines of clients**
  - **What is their story of what is happening here between you?***
  - Where might their story come from?
  - **Who might they ask you to be? How might they invite you to act?***
  - **What position might they offer you in this story?**
  - What position might they (prefer to) take? (In what storyline?)
- **Contemplating positioning and storylines of practitioner/supervisee**
  - **What is your story of what is happening here/between you?***
  - What position do you prefer to offer the other person?
  - Do you think they will accept the position you offer?
  - **How might your posture affect the positions you can/cannot take?***
  - How might your voice tone/body posture affect who you can be?
  - **How might your (age, gender, ethnicity etc.) social difference/similarity enable or constrain how you work together?***
- **Extending repertoire of positions and postures**
  - **If you adopted a different posture/tone what would you be doing? How would you do it?***
  - What other positions might you take/invite?
  - What other story could you tell of what is happening here/who you are?
  - How could you create opportunities for taking alternative positions?
  - What would enable you to keep using that tone/body posture?

Note

1 I use the word 'meeting' in this chapter to refer to all encounters with clients, supervisees, colleagues and practitioners including therapy, supervision and training sessions, consultations and management meetings.

References

Andersen, T. (ed.) (1991) *The Reflecting Team: Dialogues and Dialogues about Dialogues*. New York: Norton.

Austin, J. L. (1965) *How to Do Things with Words*. New York: Oxford University Press.

Bakhtin, M. M. (1981) *The Dialogical Imagination*. Edited by M. Holquist, trans. by C. Emerson and M. Holquist. Austin, TX: University of Texas Press.

Bakhtin, M. M. (1993) *Toward a Philosophy of the Act, with Translation and Notes by Vadim Lianpov*. Edited by M. Holquist. Austin, TX: University of Texas Press.

Burnham, J. (2005) Relational reflexivity: a tool for socially constructing therapeutic relationships. In C. Flaskas, B. Mason and A. Perlesz (eds). *The Space Between: Experience, Context and Process in the Therapeutic Relationship*. London: Karnac.

Burnham, J. (2012) Are you sitting too comfortably? Using the praxis of positioning to move between the activities of therapy-supervision and the identities of therapist supervisor. *Clinical Child Psychology and Psychiatry*, 17(2), 171–80.

Burr, V. (2003) *Social Constructionism*. 2nd Ed. London: Routledge.

Cronen, V. E. and Pearce, W. B. (1985) Toward an explanation of how the Milan Method works: an invitation to a systemic epistemology and the evolution of family systems. In D. Campbell and R. Draper (eds). *Applications of Systemic Family Therapy*. London: Grune & Strauss.

Davies, B. and Harré, R. (1990) Positioning: the discursive production of selves. *Journal for the Theory of Social Behaviour*, 20, 43–64.

Fredman, (2004) *Transforming Emotion: Conversations in Counselling and Psychotherapy*. London: Whurr/Wiley.

Fredman, G. (2007) Preparing our selves for the therapeutic relationship: revisiting 'Hypothesizing Revisited'. *Human Systems: The Journal of Systemic Consultation and Management*, 18, 44–59.

Griffith, J. L. and Elliott Griffith, M. (1994) *The Body Speaks. Therapeutic Dialogues for Mind–Body Problems*. New York: Basic Books.

Harré, R. and Van Langenhove, L. (eds) (1999) *Positioning Theory*. Oxford: Blackwell.

Shotter, J. (1993) *Conversational Realities: Constructing Life through Language*. London: Sage.

Shotter, J. (2006) Vygotsky, Bakhtin, Goethe: consciousness and the dynamics of voice. Paper given in the Department of Communication, University of California at San Diego, May 3rd, 2006.

Shotter, J. (2008) Dialogism and polyphony in organizational theorizing: action guiding anticipations and the continuous creation of novelty. *Organization Studies*, 29(4), 501–24.

Vygotsky, L. S. (1986) *Thought and Language*. Cambridge, MA: MIT Press.

6 Reflecting on power and difference in the supervision process

Glenda Fredman and Jo Bownas

In chapter 5, Glenda notes how 'words are not only heard or received but they also move the talker'. We editors both had this experience as we engaged with the chapters in Part I of this book, entitled 'Power and difference embodied in the supervision process'. We did not just see and read the words; they touched us and moved us. Our joint editing-writing process, over time, mirrored the content of the chapters: as the chapter drafts passed back and forth between each other and our author colleagues, we editors engaged personally with the author's words on each page, 'drinking them in' and noticing their effects on our bodies and our practice. In this way, we embodied the material offered in the chapters as we read them, finding ourselves experiencing strong feelings, perhaps of sadness or rage, or of elation or inspiration as we read in the moment. Over time we have found ourselves further embodying the ideas and practices presented in the chapters, sometimes as a supervisor, a practitioner, supervisee or trainee. We are grateful to the authors of Part I for the opportunity to engage personally with their writing and for their contributions to our developing supervision practice.

Nick Pendry's invitation (chapter 2) to define myself (Glenda) racially and to reflect on the meanings and the influences of my racial identity, immediately, to quote Philip Messent (chapter 3), 'turned the camera on myself' and drew me in to taking a good look at the 'part my whiteness plays' in my supervision, as a White female supervisor facing the 'inescapable reality' that I live in a 'White-dominated society' where "race" is a 'major organising principle of [our] everyday life and relationships'. Barnett Pearce's lesson came to me that:

> When a White man walks into a room he sees people. When a White woman walks into a room she sees men and women. When a Black man walks into a room he sees Black people and White people. And when a Black woman walks into a room she sees Black men and White men and Black women and White women.[1]

However, Nick Pendry's caution against using 'reductionist terms of Black and White' to classify people simply on the basis of appearance with the assumption that they share similar histories, legacies and experiences of oppression, opened space for me to pan the camera wider than my whiteness; to bring into view other contexts of my privilege and experience that have both supported and hindered my occupying preferred personal and professional positions.

As the camera zoomed in and out, like Philip Messent, I (Glenda) saw a 'complex intersection of age, gender and seniority' that brought to my mind some recent episodes in supervision with White male supervisees where interaction had gone wrong between us, and the supervisee and I were left with feelings of confusion, discomfort, hurt and unease. Philip's chapter gave me the courage to re-look at some of these past moments. In retrospect, I notice how the impact of our 'intersecting identities' contributed to interactions between us going wrong. Philip's experience highlighted that I, too, am not always conscious about the difference age makes to the way my actions or perspectives are experienced. I was the youngest child in my family, the youngest in my class at school throughout my school years, young for my year at university and hence well-practised in 'following the lead', 'looking up to' and 'knowing my place'. Slowly I grew up to being 'the same age' as the people I work with. Being 'older' and sometimes 'old' still feels like a new experience for me, and I now recognise that the more negative stories about older people in our culture have probably distracted me from acknowledging my power and privilege in the eyes of my younger male supervisees. At a time when public services are giving the message that older practitioners offer nothing extra, are 'resistant to change', are 'out-of-date', have 'not kept up' with recent trainings and are paid more than they are worth, I am frequently party, in my work context, to opinions that older practitioners are seen as less worthy or 'too expensive'. Incorporating those stories into our intersecting identities explains something of how come I have misread or perhaps misjudged how my younger, White male supervisees have positioned me as a senior teacher or 'super-visor' with power and authority to evaluate when I have positioned myself as a colleague or collaborator in a collegial or collaborative relationship.

When I bring gender into the mix of intersecting identities, alongside age and seniority differences, the possibilities for misunderstandings multiply. Having been professionally socialised in the occupations of clinical psychology and family therapy where men held, and still hold, most of the senior positions of power and authority, although women make up the majority of the workforce, I now wonder how my gender stories have informed my expectations that men expect to or even should take the lead, further contributing to my 'tendency to retreat to safe territory . . . in moments of relational danger' (Messent) even if that has meant not helping the supervisee.

Reading these chapters has encouraged me to 'linger a little' with that felt sense of 'relational danger' (Messent) and use some of the gifts I have been given from these authors to keep the conversation going. In future, I plan to name my different selves that I bring to the supervision relationship, including 'supervisor', 'woman', 'White person', 'senior practitioner' and 'older person', making visible the voices that are part of clusters of conversations we call supervision (Sharon Bond, chapter 4); invite the supervisee to engage with me so we both make visible the positions of privilege and oppression we hold in this supervision relationship;

explore how our differences intersect, and suggest we both speak from the different contexts and experiences of our privilege and oppression.

Reminded that 'conversations are relational, never finished but always emerging as one conversation overlaps with another' (Bond, chapter 4) I am left with a commitment to continue those sometimes challenging conversations in supervision; taking responsibility for the worlds I contribute to constructing in supervision (Messent), mindful that as a supervisor I hold power to perpetuate or challenge inequality (Pendry).

Like Glenda, I (Jo) found that reading the chapters in this section of the book brought many resonances for me, sending ripples of connection into the many identities of my 'multi-being' (Sharon Bond) and into distant corners of memory. Reading with my White body, these resonances and ripples were sometimes uncomfortable, but they were always generative. Nick Pendry's powerful reminder of the necessity of keeping "race" and racism on the supervision agenda, and Philip Messent's account of the sometimes painful complexity of working as a White supervisor of Black supervisees, really struck a chord with me and surfaced a long distant memory.

> I was a young and enthusiastic social worker working with many clients whose "race" or cultures were different from my own. I was drawn to the work of NAFSIYAT, the transcultural therapy centre, and eagerly took myself off to a one-day workshop there. I was the only White participant and I found myself listening to the other participants' many experiences of racism. After a while I began to feel restless and impatient, thinking, 'I know about racism, but the question is what we do as professionals.' As I began to voice this question I was met (deservedly) with angry responses, dismissing my question as testimony of my ignorance of the reality of racism. For a while I engaged with this response and then, all of a sudden, my body took over and erupted into unstoppable tears. At the time I was embarrassed and furious with myself for crying, thinking it must have appeared as an attempt to re-position myself as 'wounded victim' and to side-step the position of 'racist oppressor'.

Looking back now, I wonder if my unwelcome tears were an expression of my body's 'knowing' first what I had not yet fully apprehended, as Sharon Bond describes in chapter 4. As in Sharon's examples, my body was perhaps responding to an experience of dissonance, in which my story of myself and what I stood for was being painfully challenged in my interaction with the workshop participants. My body was perhaps also registering an intense '*knowing from*' (Shotter, 1993) the other participants' experience (familiar to them) of being marginalised and dismissed; a 'knowing' that was very different to my naïvely assumed '*knowing about*' racism. By shaking me with tears, my wise body stopped my words for a while, humbling and quietening me so that I re-entered the conversation in a different position, prepared for really listening and reflecting.

Bringing this memory, stirred by reading the chapters in Part I, to my current identity as supervisor of therapists and clinicians, I find that these chapters offer me many future possibilities. I remember that, when the tears of my younger self subsided, I realised that I had been asking the wrong question: instead of asking 'what do *we* do?' I should have been asking 'what do *I* do' (as a White person). Nick Pendry holds me firmly to this question, reminding me of the pervasive presence of racism and how passive acceptance of the privileges of my whiteness perpetuates the diminishing effects of racism in the lives of others. I hope that a regular re-reading of his chapter may act as something of an antidote to this passivity. Glenda Fredman's chapter offers me a beautiful answer to the question of 'what do *I* do?' She writes of how she invites practitioners to prepare *themselves* for the therapeutic relationship by attending to how they might use their own bodies and voices to position them and the people they are meeting with. I am particularly drawn to Glenda's reference to Bakhtin's (1981) idea that we 'populate' our words with feelings and intentions; and it occurs to me that, for people familiar with experiences of marginalisation, our professional voices may be populated with ghosts of earlier oppressors. Following Glenda's work, in future I will invite supervisees to reflect on the stories they are telling about the people with whom they are to meet, how these stories may shape their bodies and tone of voice and what kind of relationship such postures could invite, including relationships of differential power. Anticipating how our clients may be feeling (taking account of their social identities and ours), and what they would like to be appreciated for as they meet with us, may then open up choices about how we might use our bodily posture and tone of voice to decline the privileges of our personal and professional identities.

I found myself connecting Glenda's practice with Sharon's exploration of how we embody the different 'domains' we work in. I thought of my own work setting, in a secure hospital. Though my own and my supervisees' intentions may be to work in the therapeutic *domain of explanation*, we embody the processes of authority and judgement associated with the *domain of production* as we steer families through search procedures and locked doors, opened by the keys we carry on our belts. These processes embody relationships of power, which may have distancing and disabling resonances for the people with whom we meet. This form of embodiment is particularly stark in our setting, but I think it has echoes in the processes of other professional settings, with their reception desks and waiting rooms, forms and clip boards. My reading of Sharon's and Glenda's work influences me to reflect with my supervisees on what we embody as we interact with our working environment; how that embodiment might be experienced by the people we meet with; and how, in the *domain of aesthetics*, we could prepare our bodies and voices to invite rewarding relationships while we do what we have to do to fulfil our professional obligations within our agencies.

Philip Messent's and Nick Pendry's chapters drew my attention to how racism and other forms of differential privilege influence our relationships, not only with clients, but also with supervisees. I was struck by Philip's example of his request, to his first Bangladeshi trainee, to 'tone down' his warm and attentive style of greeting clients in order to fit with the culture of the agency. Philip makes me think again about how our practices of therapy are embedded in dominant cultures; and how we can seek to replicate these cultures (and their dominance) in training and supervision. I wonder about the times when, in my own practice, I may have used the power associated with my membership of the dominant culture to prescribe practices that were at odds with my supervisee's embodiment (to sit closer or further apart; to speak louder or quieter; to interrupt more or less; to be more or less physically active; to be more or less formal and so on). And I reflect on how I have done this, without pausing to deconstruct the cultural contexts that gave rise to my prescriptions; to consider that I may be asking the supervisee to change the very way her identity is constituted in her body; or to consider what ***I*** could learn from deconstructing ***my*** familiar practices in the context of ***her*** culture.

Learning from his early experience, Philip goes on to introduce his current practice of mutually sharing, between supervisor and supervisee, their respective cultural styles of relating. I recall a recently qualified supervisee asking my help to 'be less wooden, to connect more with the people I am meeting'. Moved by Philip's chapter, if I re-imagine that supervision episode now, picturing myself, a White, female supervisor, working with a Black, male supervisee, I wonder if I might first need to deconstruct my own 'White, British, older woman' solutions to the question of 'connecting'. Perhaps I would do that quietly in my own inner talk or perhaps I would speak out loud: 'When I feel I am being "wooden" in therapy I sometimes move into "just chatting" for a while with the family; or I might move a little closer to the family; or join the children on the floor; or I might introduce humour. Those are things I find I can do in my particular body, as an older White, British woman, things that fit with ways of being from my family and culture. But I think there are many different ways of "connecting" and some of them are not possible for me.' I might go on to ask my supervisee: 'Could you picture yourself now connecting with your own family, with your close friends or your community?' 'What would I see your body doing (Afuape, chapter 7) that would show me you were connecting?' 'Which of those ways of using your body to connect would fit for you with your ideas about being a therapist?' 'If those ways of using your body do not fit with your ideas of being a therapist, where do you think those ideas come from?' 'Might they be influenced by White men's or by women's ways of being a therapist?' 'If you were to be a "connecting" therapist in your own body, what might that look like?'

Coming full circle, I (Jo) return to that memory of my younger self experiencing the shock of having my preferred identity stories challenged by my fellow workshop participants. In my later positions as supervisor and trainer, I have met with White supervisees and trainees who have not yet become aware of the unearned privilege associated with their whiteness. They may acknowledge the possibility that racism affects the lives of their clients, and they may have good intentions to address this in their work; but they may still struggle to put themselves into the picture. I understand that struggle, I know it myself. To contemplate that I may be a participant or beneficiary in the suffering of others brings a unique pain to the centre of my body, and a wish to stop the thought that causes such a pain. Sharon Bond's innovative development of the *domain of rhetoric* offers me a way forward in working with these struggles. Sharon suggests that in order to know how to 'go on' in a problematic situation we may first need to '*give account*' of our selves and our actions in a way that both addresses our audiences and is coherent with our own identity stories. I think of those supervisees who are struggling to put the power and privilege of their own whiteness into the picture of their work. Inspired by Sharon's work, I might now invite them first to consider the stories they tell about themselves, their values and abilities. I might wonder with them how those stories might be interrupted by considering their own power and privilege; and how their bodies respond to these dissonances. I might then explore with them the development of an 'account' that could make room for all that their white identity means, whilst being coherent with the familiar and preferred stories of their intentions, abilities and values. Together we might then consider how such an account allows the supervisee to 'go on': the actions that flow from the account giving.

Reading the chapters in this part of the book brought to mind the writing of educationalist bel hooks (1994: 137), whose idea that 'the person who is the most powerful has the power of denying their body' influenced us greatly when we first read it. hooks proposes that 'we must return ourselves to a state of embodiment in order to de-construct the way power has been traditionally orchestrated in the classroom' (p. 139). The chapters in Part I prompt us to think how this is relevant to the therapy classroom and the supervision room. As White women, supervisors and trainers we are often in the position of being the one with 'the power to deny my body' and these chapters both remind us of this and offer some wonderful ways forward. We want to thank the authors for the places they have taken us and for the future possibilities they have opened up.

Note

1 I have not been able to find this 'lesson' in any of Barnett Pearce's writing and am not sure if he adapted it from someone else's writing.

References

Bakhtin, M. M. (1981) *The Dialogical Imagination.* Edited by M. Holquist, trans. by C. Emerson and M. Holquist. Austin, TX: University of Texas Press.

hooks, b. (1994) *Teaching to Transgress: Education as the Practice of Freedom.* London: Routledge.

Shotter, J. (1993). *Conversational Realities: Constructing Life Through Language.* London: Sage.

Part II

Using our bodies with intention in supervision

7 Supervision as relational responsivity

The body in co-ordinated meaning making

Taiwo Afuape

> I saw some piglets suckling their dead mother. After a short while they shuddered and went away . . . what they loved in their mother wasn't her body, but whatever it was that made her body live.
>
> (Confucius, 551–497 BC: in Kleiser, 2005)

In this chapter, I explore supervision as relational responsivity by highlighting a social constructionist approach to embodiment, namely Co-ordinated Management of Meaning (CMM). I have tried to find a balance between describing my practice so that it is comprehendible whilst not telling you, the reader, how to do it, as that would contradict the notion of relational responsivity being what emerges bodily in the unique moment, rather than anything that can be pre-conceived.

It feels important to start this chapter by introducing myself, my complex relationship with my body and my approach to supervision.

> As a child I was an elective mute. Unlike my sociable twin sister, I did not speak to people outside of my family I was not close to. Following a psychological assessment, my parents were told that I would always have difficulty talking. My parents responded by politely explaining that there was nothing wrong with me; I was 'just shy'. And they were right. I was sensitive, socially awkward, self-conscious and creative. I would write and draw anywhere I could; often ripping off bits of wallpaper in my bedroom to write on the beige underside. Sharing a bed with my twin sister, I once woke up from a wonderful dream, picked up a pen and started to draw the angels from my dream on my plain white pillow-case. My brother and eldest sister, who were checking on us, found me with my pillow case covered in angels. My eldest sister took the pillowcase from me, replaced it with a patterned one and told me to not draw on it and to go back to sleep. The next day I saw my angel-covered pillowcase hanging on her bedroom wall. I was fortunate enough

to come from a family where my ways of being and expressing myself were validated and acknowledged; even when they did not involve spoken words.

**

In August 2012, I woke from a major operation feeling elated, as though my body knew that something that I had been living with, that made me unwell, had been removed. I also felt a strong desire to have a pen. A few nurses looked for a pen for me but explained that pens were a scarce resource on hospital wards as they often went missing. Although I did not want to bother the wonderful nurses with something so small, I had a feeling in my body that this need for a pen was not trivial. When one nurse finally found a pen and cheerfully gave it to me I experienced an instant feeling of relief and ease in my body; a palpable 'felt sense' that I had something important in my hand.

My body, my contexts

I am from a family that is proud and embodied. We are very tactile, affectionate and expressive. We love to dance, we hug each other, we hold hands, we touch each other's faces, we jump with joy, we wave our hands and shout when angry and we double over when we laugh. My parents are from Nigeria, a culture that encourages embodiment (being present and alive to our bodily felt experience). The most visible sign of this is the way in which babies are strapped to the backs of mothers and other significant carers. As my friends are also tactile, I am surrounded by people who value spontaneous qualities of bodily expression.

Being seriously ill a few years ago was undoubtedly challenging, but it also left me with much gratitude for my body and its determination to heal. A systemic therapist (Adriana Penalosa-Clarke) I was seeing at that time, commented that I seemed a 'much happier, freer and more spontaneous' person when I was 'in [my] body' than when I was 'locked inside [my] head'. This reflection resonated with me as I was discovering that I was a Buddhist, and had started a meditation and yoga practice.

Coming from a political family background where I was surrounded by Anti-discrimination, Afrocentric, Feminist and Socialist ideas, I have always been a critical thinker and committed to ethical and empowering practice in all aspects of my work and interaction with others. Therefore, when I trained as a clinical psychologist and systemic therapist, I selected courses that emphasised social constructionist critiques of mainstream practice and for over 13 years I have been committed to developing community, systemic, preventative, early intervention and liberation psychology approaches, which work to actively address inequality, oppression and injustice.

The embodied and disembodied world

Oppression and the body

The Minority world[1] (Europe, Canada, North America and Australia) often views embodied cultures as inferior to cultures that emphasise the use of our minds. Although we cannot really separate a thinking mind from a responsive body, I am writing here as though we can, in order to highlight how the Minority world often negatively connotes embodiment. For example, I have heard comments like 'those Africans are good at singing and dancing but not much else', which mirrors how body-based cultures (from Africa, Asia, the Middle East and Latin America) are treated as backward, albeit exotic, quaint and entertaining. In addition, embodiment is commonly associated with childhood and femininity in cultures that subjugate women and children.

In my experience oppression can disturb authentic bodily expression and the connection with our bodies we are born with. Being Black and a woman means that I am oppressed merely because I have a body. My physical appearance is often linked with prejudices and viewed as 'not mainstream' (for example, my natural hair) and I am dehumanised by the sexist tendency to value female bodies for how they look rather than the myriad other qualities they possess. Being defined by and reduced to my body has at times left me with a distant relationship with it, in order to redefine my worth; as if to communicate, '*I am a mind, not just a body*'. In this way, oppression encourages me to be hyperaware of my presence in a way that can be constraining of my ability to just *be*. Consequently, I can find myself neglecting the sensational side of experience and living inside my head as I try to navigate my way around confusing messages and subtle exclusion.

Much of the literature on addressing power in supervision refers to what I call 'heady' activities, such as '*interrogating* interconnected social identities that shape power dynamics in supervisory relationships' and 'critical *analysis*' which involves '*unveiling* . . . structural . . . and relational power' and '*questioning*' the status quo (Hernández and McDowell, 2010: 29 – my emphasis added). Riikonen (1999) states that what makes dialogue 'inspiring, meaningful, or resonating', cannot be understood in any purely cognitive or rational way. Despite our preconceived plans to create good interactions, it mostly happens in the moment as a result of responsiveness and awareness. Given the increasing subtlety of oppression and prejudice, we might need to focus on our subtle ways of being, in order to be more receptive to each other. Developing body-based approaches to supervision adds something important to a head-based approach, so that we can reflect on *what we are creating together,* with an understanding that what we create is always an embodied (and not just a linguistic) process.

Responsivity and the body

Responsivity involves being fully-present and spontaneous within the process as it happens rather than 'stepping out' in order to think about the experience from the outside. In Buddhism, the mind is seen as part of a whole system of being and includes all aspects of experience, such as bodily sensations (unlike the Minority world view of 'mind' consisting of conscious thoughts separate from the body). In *Pāḷi*, the language of the earliest Buddhist scriptures, there is no distinction between thinking and feeling and '*citta*' (pronounced chitta) means 'heart-mind'. Buddhists refer to feeling as '*vedanā*' which is a '*felt sense*', the unclear, pre-verbal sense of something experienced in the body. It is not the same as an emotion, but rather a bodily sense of the *total* emotional situation, of many things together, in which an emotion can be embedded or from which an emotion might emerge (Gendlin, 2003). When I was given a pen in the hospital I experienced a '*felt sense*' rather than an emotion.

Meditation involves focusing on this sort of *felt sense,* through absorption and engagement, in order to cultivate awareness of how we are in our body, speech and mind. In the same way, we are absorbed by a beautiful painting or poem, we spend time being absorbed by and in our bodies, which leads to being full of the immediate experience. I have found that practising yoga, in a similar way, connects me to a bodily knowing and awareness different from a 'head-based' knowing. If I connect to what I am doing in a more cognitive way I come out of meditation and lose balance. Any difficult feelings I have at the start of a yoga session *always* shift in a very physical way by the end of the session. It is not just that I feel more relaxed; if I am pre-occupied by something that I cannot dissolve rationally, without fail, a resolution comes to me that I did not have before, and helps me move on. It is as though yoga practice allows something useful to float up from a bodily sense, by bypassing the confused clutter of the mind.

Thus, meditation that involves focused attention, cultivating compassion, kindly awareness and embodiment is a way of being more fully present in the world rather than an escape from it. As a supervisor, who wants to embody my ethical commitment to being fully present to another person in ways they find helpful rather than oppressive, I have found this approach to awareness and absorption, which integrates thinking and feeling, central to how supervision can be relationally responsive.

Supervision as a relationally responsive and dialogical practice

Relational responsivity refers to the ways in which participants in interaction respond to the actions and feelings of each other, by being fully present in the relationship. Relational responsivity, therefore, involves focusing on moment-to-moment experience and being struck by what emerges (Shotter and Katz, 1999), in a way that opens up avenues for new action (Lowe, 2005). When I have participated in this sort of relational, responsive and collaborative process, supervision has offered me much more than just additional knowledge or skills, and has engaged my whole being, with a palpable shift in my *felt sense*, and not just my mind.

The supervisors who have most influenced me and my approach to being a supervisor have drawn on social constructionist approaches such as CMM

(Cronen and Pearce, 1985). To fully appreciate a social constructionist approach to supervision, it has been helpful for me to reflect on the distinctions between the philosophical worldviews of positivism, constructivism and social constructionism, and their different implications for how we understand the world and activities such as supervision.

Positivism posits that reality has an objective quality; things have an essence and knowledge is an accurate and verifiable description of things as they really are. It is, therefore, possible to have unbiased and direct access to reality and use language to describe what actually exists. This worldview sees client-systems in fixed, structural terms, operating in ways that can be viewed objectively by the therapist as either functional or dysfunctional. The therapist is outside of the client-system, and the supervisor, as an objective observer, is outside of the therapist–client-system looking in. Hence, positivist supervision involves a hierarchical relationship that assumes supervisors have privileged access to knowledge and experience that enables them to make expert judgements and teach supervisees about the right course of action. This perspective encourages 'purposive action on the part of the supervisor' and interventions in supervision that 'are carefully planned and deliberate' (Hernández-Wolfe, 2010: 290).

Constructivism posits that every person uniquely constructs their reality; knowledge is something that develops within an individual, and we use language to describe our unique perception of the world. Therefore, there are as many versions of reality (multiversa) as there are observers to view reality (Maturana and Varela, 1980). Hence, in supervision informed by constructivism, supervisors view themselves as part of the therapy–supervision system, with the therapist/supervisee and client, and join supervisees in generating multiple perspectives. The supervisor also supports the supervisee to reflect on their unique perception (self-reflexivity), and how their ways of seeing shapes their interaction with clients.

Social constructionism assumes that the social world is not objectively discovered, but created through social interaction (Pearce, 2007) whereby wider social forces shape individuals and the individual shapes the world (Burr, 2003). This perspective challenges the quest for, and belief in, ultimate truths, approaching meanings as not static and unchanging, but fluid and dynamic as they are developed in social interaction and within multiple levels of context. Meaning is never complete because there are always new ideas and new ways of looking at old ideas (Anderson and Goolishian, 1990). Mindful of the relationship between power and knowledge (Gardner *et al.*, 1997), supervisors informed by a social constructionist approach move away from the position of scientist-practitioner and teacher, who gives answers or opinions, to the reflexive responsive position of supervisors, who offer suggestions and reflections that invite feedback from supervisees about what is useful. The search for the right way is replaced by the idea that different views emerge from different contexts and bring opportunities to, and impose constraints on, our lives. This process of collaboration, co-creation and reflexivity makes sense of the intimacy I have experienced in a social constructionist approach to supervision.

Since supervisors and therapists are an 'integral part of the therapeutic system' (Hernández-Wolfe, 2010: 293), what supervisors embody has further reaching implications than just what happens in the supervisory relationship. Hence, supervisees have often told me that my way of being in supervision enables them to be more curious, open to otherness and receptive with their clients. In social constructionist supervision, therefore, the supervisor joins with supervisees to co-construct new stories and types of storytelling that are useful to supervisees and the people with whom they work (Pearce and Pearce, 1998). Given that the body is central to the storytelling process, the body is an important level of context in the dialogue.

The body as an important level of context

When we are born we experience and react to the world pre-verbally in ways that are direct, immediate and physical. As we become verbal our experience is subject to thought, and we might forget that there are other sorts of experience. In the Minority world, the body has largely been viewed as a commodity and consumer, a distraction from the superior expressions of the mind and a machine that either works well or breaks down. If the body is an object, a distraction or a machine, it makes sense that we would not view it as being able to offer us new understanding and meaning.

Cronen and Pearce's (1985) CMM theory includes the body as one of the contexts making up our social world (see figure 7.1). Cronen and Pearce describe how we act out of and into multiple contexts that include the body. There are stories connected to our contexts that inform the meanings we give to our actions, relationships and beliefs. Thus, CMM throws light on the processes of both how we make meaning *and* co-ordinate our (embodied) actions with each other.

The levels of contexts out of which we act are not fixed and can change, the highest level of context will depend on what is the strongest contextual force in any given moment. Lower level contexts can still exert a profound, albeit weaker (implicative), force on meaning and action. Thus, CMM highlights the contextual nature of our embodiment, how multiple levels of context shape our embodiment as well as how our bodily experience can shape our contexts. By acknowledging that our bodies are an intrinsic part of the storytelling process, through which we make meaning and co-ordinate our actions, CMM offers a useful framework for understanding how embodiment can open up and constrain possibilities in supervision (Pearce, 2007).

Approaching body in supervision

Since changing the context will change the meaning (Bateson, 1978), engaging with different levels of context can open up new connections and avenues for action. I try to introduce reflections from contexts that are 'appropriately unusual' enough to promote new perspectives (Hernández-Wolfe, 2010: 295) and yet not

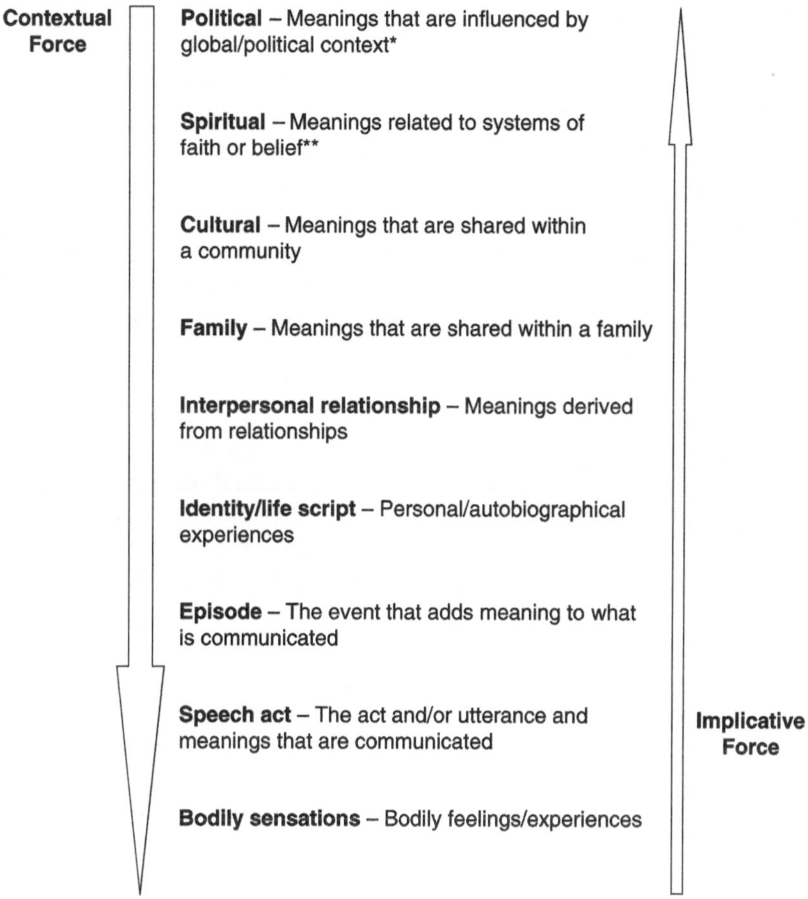

Figure 7.1 CMM Levels of Context

Source: Afuape (2011)'s depiction of 'Levels of Context', adapted from Pearce (2007).
* Addition made by Nimisha Patel, November 2005 personal communication. ** Addition made by Karen Partridge, May 2007 personal communication.

so unusual that they disengage, confuse or distress supervisees. Given the Minority world's relative lack of attention to the body, I take care to introduce the context of, and reflections on, embodiment in supervision in ways that introduce the difference that makes the difference, without being too different (Bateson, 1972). I usually start by asking the supervisee permission to attend to the body by saying something like, 'I am someone who believes that what happens in the body can be a useful area to explore in supervision. Is it okay if I ask questions in relation to this belief?' With agreement, I go on to ask questions that connect to their embodied experience, for example, 'You say you felt [anxious and overwhelmed] in that moment. What tends to happen in your body when you feel like that?'

'How does that way of being in your body impact on how you are in the room with others?' 'How do other people seem to respond to you when you do that?'

> In a supervision session, an older, White British, female supervisee, Patricia, held herself tight around her stomach as she related the extensive trauma history of a woman with whom she was working. Patricia said she was 'trying not to cry'. I put my hands between my stomach and my chest and asked her, 'If you pay attention to that part of your body, what do you notice there?' She said it felt 'knotted in the centre . . . with an empty space around it'. When I asked about the quality of the knot and of the space, the phrase that came to her was 'alone with my tears'.[2]

As therapists and supervisors, we have been socialised to use particular words in particular situations and to be embodied in particular ways in our therapeutic practice depending on the situation we are in and the cultural (including professional) rules we live and work by. Embodied aspects of our talk, such as where we sit, when or if ever we make physical contact and how we respond when people cry, are often informed by social discourses coming from professional, cultural or family contexts (Fredman, 2004). Since the invitation to foreground the context of her body seemed to fit comfortably for Patricia, I continued with 'body talk'.

> The space between my stomach and chest also felt knotted. Despite this connection, the physical distance between us felt disconnecting. I asked Patricia if she was okay with where I was sitting or if she wanted me to be closer. She said she wanted me to sit with her, so I sat alongside her holding her hand.

A responsive, embodied, dialogical approach to supervision involves co-creating with others what responses make the most sense, are most comfortable and acceptable to them in the moment with respect to different levels of context. My enquiring about the physical distance between us seemed to invite Patricia to notice and articulate that she wanted more proximity than was usual for us in supervision.

Using CMM to guide my enquiry, I went on to invite Patricia to reflect with me on the impact of our contexts (in bold) on our preferences for bodily closeness with questions like: 'In my **family culture** we tend to want to be close to people who are upset so I might forget to ask what other people's preference is. How has your experience of your **family and/or friends** contributed to your ideas about physical closeness when you/others are upset? How do your **personal experiences** shape your preferences? How do your preferences fit with the **culture(s)** you grew up in? How do your **professional training/spiritual** beliefs inform your preference for closeness/distance? What difference does **gender** make to your ideas and preferences? How have your ideas changed over **time**?

How do these ideas influence your **clinical practice**? What aspect of this experience might you bring into, or offer up, in the relationship with the client we have been discussing?'

Including the body in meaning making in supervision

When reviewing videotaped therapy sessions with supervisees, supervisors commonly ask questions about the underlying assumptions, theories or ideas guiding supervisees in particular moments, which usually brings forth supervisees' professional theories or personal stories from their family, relationship or cultural contexts. To bring forth the body context, I often add, in the spirit of kindly, rather than critical, awareness, questions about bodily experience ('What do you notice in your body?') and their meaning for the therapeutic relationship ('Do you think [the client] notices?' 'What effect is that having on how you can be with [the client]?' 'What is that making possible/constraining between you?'). My aim is not to define any particular bodily positioning as right or wrong, but to reflect on the possible impact on the therapeutic relationship with respect to power, in order to open up new avenues for action. Including the body as a context for co-ordinating our meaning making often calls attention to our taken-for-granted ways of being in our bodies that have become invisible to our awareness, as happened with Paul in the following example.

> Paul, a White English, middle-class, male supervisee, described having difficulties engaging a White English, working-class mother (Mrs K), whom he experienced as 'overbearing'. Reviewing videotape with Paul after the session, I noticed that he often held up his hand in front of Mrs K when she spoke over her child. When we explored his hand gesture with questions such as 'what was your intention when . . .?' and 'why is this important to you?', Paul explained his desire to 'make sure the child had a voice' in the session. He reflected that he would have liked 'the power to pause' his own parents when he was younger. When I asked what he was hoping for in his work with this child's mother, he explained that he also wanted Mrs K to 'feel heard and respected' by him, which opened space for us to consider the opportunities and constraints of this hand gesture from the mother's point of view in light of her experience of abuse from male partners.

Kindly awareness

Given the critical gaze on bodies in the wider cultural context, an atmosphere of *kindly awareness* is a necessary context for inviting reflection on embodiment in supervision.

Observing with the spirit of *kindly awareness* is so important that I may forgo a video review if supervisees do not feel they can observe themselves in my presence in a way that will be enabling and helpful, rather than disabling or undermining.

> This gentle exploration, in which I held a posture of kindly awareness with Paul, gave him confidence to mention to the family that he had noticed, when viewing the videotape with his supervisor, his tendency to hold his hand up to Mrs K. He wondered what this was like for her. Mrs K said that she 'understood why' he did it, although it did make her 'feel uncomfortable and a bit put down'. Paul shared his cultural assumptions about the importance of giving voice to the child. He went on to explore how the family's beliefs and stories regarding 'giving voice to the child', from their cultural, community and family contexts, gave meaning to their experiences and shaped their behaviour with each other.
>
> When Mrs K and her son agreed that a child 'having a voice' was important to them too, Paul was able to ask how they wanted to be 'paused' in the conversation, opening space for the boy to suggest employing 'a pretend remote control' that all of them could use in the sessions, 'and even take home'.

Bringing preferred ways of being to body

Sometimes supervisees have described feeling that social meanings ascribed to their bodies constrain their co-ordination with clients.

> Margaret, a Black British female supervisee, told me she felt 'too stiff' in sessions working with a family with small children. She had attended a workshop where a White male psychiatrist had shown examples of his 'amazing playful practice' with children. Margaret said, 'But I can't be him. I'm a Black woman in a skirt. I think I would feel ridiculous.' When I invited Margaret to describe how she would prefer to be with the parents and the children in this family, she explained that she wanted to be much 'riskier' and 'braver' in sessions.

To enable supervisees to embody the ethics, style or ways of being they value, I draw on questions informed by the Narrative approach (White, 2004) to explore who in their life, past and present, most embodies their preferred style of being.

> I asked Margaret, 'Who comes to mind as a good example of this way of being "brave" and "risky" you would like to develop?' She immediately mentioned her previous Latin American female supervisor. When I asked, 'What would I see in her body that would help me notice she was being brave?' Margaret explained that she was 'not afraid to express herself

> through her body', for example, 'express herself with her hands'. As she spoke, Margaret allowed her hands to become animated, noting that this was a familiar way of expressing herself in her family but she did not feel she had the freedom to 'risk' it emerging in a professional context. Being given permission in supervision to be 'braver', and reconnect to the resources in her family cultural context, made it possible for Margaret to join the young children in their embodiment spontaneously in the next family session; by sitting with them on low chairs at their level, she created a context for the emergence of talk about social oppression and prejudice that had not happened before.

The process of writing this chapter and engaging with, and learning from, the editors of this volume, has enabled me to reflect on further questions that I could have asked the supervisee. For instance: 'Does your self like your hands doing that?' and 'What do your moving hands make possible for you here?' Asking questions like this could have invited Margaret to reflect on what she found easier to say and do as a result of her different embodiment and further enriched the process of supervision as well as the client–therapist relationship.

Supervision can provide an opportunity for us to extend or develop our bodily repertoire in practice, and to experiment with different ways of using and being in our bodies. Inviting supervisees to explore how they might bring their preferred ways of being not just to mind, but specifically to body, has been useful with supervisees like Margaret and with other practitioners who value and want to have a richer appreciation of what they are doing in their bodies when in relationship with clients.

Coherence, co-ordination and mystery in supervision

When we meet others, we do so with and in our bodies (Shotter, 2010). The Majority world tends to view the body as a process and part of other natural living processes. Therefore, the body is perceived not only as receiver of and vehicle for the non-verbal, non-rational and subtle aspects of experience, but also as an important context for our storytelling, meaning making and co-ordination.

Coherence

It is much easier for supervision to run smoothly when supervisor and supervisee share a common framework and their approaches fit; when there is coherence between the stories that inform their approach to therapy and supervision. This was not the case with Marco and me.

> A middle-class, White Italian, male supervisee, Marco, had opposing political views from mine. Whenever I used social constructionist ideas

> in his supervision he called them 'political' and 'unscientific'. Despite intending to remain questioning, humble and curious, I found myself in a verbal tussle with Marco in every supervision session.

The story I was telling myself about the type of supervisor I was and wanted to be (facilitating, reflexive, kindly aware) was not coherent with the story I was living (critical, judgemental, argumentative) in interaction with Marco. Increasingly, I did not like the person I was being in supervision. I felt tense, nervous and a little sick in my stomach before each session. There was also a dissonance between my emotional posture and ethical stance, since readying myself to feel attacked further entrenched me in my defensive judgemental position. I swung between questioning *my* competence to questioning Marco's; neither position was helpful in supporting us to co-ordinate. Every time I told myself 'it's okay . . . stay curious, listen more' my body's response to 'it's okay' was to feel more sick. In fact, Gendlin said that one way to 'let the felt sense come' is to say, in a situation that is not okay, 'everything is fine' (Gendlin and Heuman, 2011: 45).

Co-ordinating meaning and actions

In my own supervision, I felt heard in a non-judgemental way as my supervisor and I reflected on the complexity of power in my supervisory relationship with Marco, with respect to gender, skin colour, class and position. Reflecting on my multiple levels of context (in bold), I was able to consider the personal experiences I brought to the situation. For example, in **my family** we are all very close, care very passionately and deeply for each other *and* we argue a lot. Despite my intentions not to engage in arguments I can find myself in them anyway! Becoming reflexive to my own contexts and meanings, I realised that when it comes to issues close to my heart, what I end up doing in conversations might be very different from my intentions. Although I intended to act according to the ethical positions informed by my **systemic therapy** and **Buddhist** contexts, my **experience** of being invalidated through **social oppression**, my **bodily** context and what happens in my **family** context exerted much stronger contextual forces so that my actions were not coherent with **my preferred way of being**.

Reflecting on the logic of my meanings and actions in this way helped to move me from a self-concerned position, whereby I was reducing Marco to my embodied experience of him, to a curious and other-oriented position in which I was able to be interested in his values and assumptions about learning and supervision. My supervisor wondered how I might change the structure of supervision with Marco to incorporate reflecting processes so that Marco and I did not invite oppositional responses from each other. I also went away thinking about the importance of preparing my body to be in line with the shifts in my thinking that occurred in my supervision.

Mystery: using 'Focusing' to bring forth new contexts

Before the next session with Marco I spent 15 minutes *Focusing*[3] (Gendlin, 2003), which involved trying to hold an open, non-judgemental, kind attention to my internal experience, which did not yet have words, in order to go down into *felt sense*, spend time with it, learn something new and ask it questions. Rather than trying to analyse, solve or make a decision using my rational mind, *Focusing* involved searching for what my experience felt like in the body and listening in a way I did not normally listen; that is, listening to what came from the *felt sense* (Gendlin, 2003). '*Implicit knowing*' is Gendlin's term for what someone knows but is not yet able to express. In order to help the *felt sense* form, I tried out words that might express it until there was some sort of fit with the *felt sense* that enabled it to shift in a helpful way. (See Exercise 7.1 for a guide to this practice.)

> As I sat with myself, Focusing, reflecting on the sick feeling in my stomach, a visual image came to me of an argument with an ex-boyfriend, in which I challenged him to put a desire to connect with me over his need to be right. The sick feeling in my stomach seemed to signify the hypocrisy of not embodying that sentiment myself. I tried to cultivate compassion for myself, my ex-boyfriend, the supervisee and the ways in which we all might feel the need to defend values important to us, as the sick feeling softened.

As a result of this bodily felt shift I entered into supervision with Marco with a different emotional posture, of openness and genuine curiosity, which meant that I listened to Marco the way I might listen to engaging music, with my whole being, and, in turn, he listened to me. Despite the difference in our views, we were able to engage with each other with less tension and more laughter.

More on mystery

Rather than happening in the moments where we manage to focus on the breath and body, meditation actually occurs in the moments where we notice we have drifted off and we *come back* to the breath. Despite what I might tell myself about the type of supervisor I hope I am and want to be, being attuned to bodily experiences makes me more aware of those moments when I drift away from this ideal, and this awareness helps bring me back. Something almost mysterious can emerge in interaction when the body is centralised. This *mystery* (Pearce, 2007) reminds us that there is far more to life than what is under rational, conscious control and understanding and points to the significance of the intangible and subtle aspects of experience.

Further reflections

Minority world culture often treats bodies as objects of gaze and as machines. Despite this vigilance, bodies are rarely seen in light of their creative and generative qualities. Treating the body as a machine is dangerous because a machine has no life in it and, as Wittgenstein (1953: 3) puts it: 'our attitude to what is alive and to what is dead is not the same'. In my everyday life, I often discount my bodily experience (for example, not going to bed when tired or eating in a hurried way at work). My working self is less and less aware of my body and more and more caught up in the endless chatter in my head, full of things I need to do and ways I need to think. Given the way I am encouraged to think of bodily senses as an unimportant background to my life, I have to actively find ways, through meditation, yoga and *Focusing*, to tune into my body, as an internally complex system (one of the most elaborate systems there are) as well as 'a wonderfully intricate interaction with everything around [it], which is why it "knows" so much just [by] being' (Gendlin, 1978: vii).

We live situations with bodies that sense much more than we might think. Disconnecting from our bodies potentially shrinks experience to what is in our head, while tuning into the body allows us to reconnect with important aspects of ourselves; as Gendlin puts it: 'I hear from the *"me"* that *"I"* don't know so well' (Gendlin, 2012: 79). Feeling less alienated from ourselves we are more likely to connect more fully with others. Supervision based on curiosity, kindly awareness and an understanding of the embodied nature of collaboration that integrates the thinking mind and responsive body, becomes *embodied connection* that is deeply felt because we are physically moved as well as mentally stimulated.

Before we end, I invite you to *Focus* on how you are leaving this chapter and how this chapter leaves you, with Exercise 7.1.

Exercise 7.1 Focusing

- *Relaxing* – Turning your attention to body, ask yourself: What comes *there* when I ask 'How am I?'
- *Felt sense* – Rather than trying to analyse, solve or make a decision using your rational mind, search for what it feels like in your body.
  Go down into your *felt sense* in this moment, spend time with it, learn something new and ask it questions.
- *Handle* – Explore the quality of this *felt sense* by letting a word, phrase or image come up from it.
  Instead of trying to impose words to make them fit the *felt sense*, listen to what comes from the *felt sense*.
- *Resonating* – In order to help the *felt sense* form, try out words (or images) that might express it. Go back and forth between the *felt sense* and the word (phrase or image) to check how they resonate with each other, until there is some sort of fit with the *felt sense* that enables it to shift in a helpful way.
- *Asking* – You might want to ask the *felt sense* questions about what it is and what it might need.
- *Receiving* – Receive whatever happens in a kindly way.

Source: Grendlin, 2003

Notes

1 Like Ani (1994), I refer to Western culture as Minority culture since Europeans and the cultures they have created represent a minority in global terms, and those of Africa, Asia, the Far East, the Middle East and Latin America as Majority cultures, since they make up the majority of the world (Afuape, 2011).

2 Practice examples of supervision are amalgamations of different experiences that have been written up in such a way as to ensure confidentiality. In particular, identifying information has been changed.

3 Focusing (Gendlin, 2003) can be done with a listener or alone and can, among other things, be used to:

- orientate our emotional posture and embody our ethical stance
- help us connect to the supervisee in supervision
- help us support the supervisee to become clearer on what they feel or want from a situation.

References

Afuape, T. (2011) *Power, Resistance and Liberation in Therapy with Survivors of Trauma: to Have our Hearts Broken.* London: Routledge.

Anderson, H. and Goolishian, H. (1990) Beyond cybernetics: comments on Atkinson and Heath's 'further thoughts on second-order family therapy'. *Family Process*, 29, 157–63.

Ani, M. (1994) *Yurugu: An African-centred Critique of European Cultural Thought and Behaviour.* New Jersey: Africa World Press.

Bateson, G. (1972) *Steps to an Ecology of the Mind.* Chicago: University of Chicago Press.

Bateson, G. (1978) The pattern which connects. *Coevolution Quarterly*, 18, 5–15.

Burr, V. (2003) *Social Constructionism*. 2nd Ed. London: Routledge.

Confucius (2005) In *Dictionary of Proverbs*. Edited by G. Kleiser. New Dehli: A.P.H. Publishing Corporation.

Cronen, V. E. and Pearce, W. B. (1985) Towards an explanation of how the Milan Method works: an invitation to a systemic epistemology and the evolution of family systems. In D. Campbell and R. Draper (eds). *Applications of Systemic Family Therapy: The Milan Approach.* London: Grune and Stratton.

Fredman, G. (2004) *Transforming Emotion: Conversations in Counselling and Psychotherapy*. London: Whurr.

Gardner, G., Bobele, M. and Biever, J. L. (1997) Postmodern models of Family Therapy supervision. In T. Todd and C.L. Storm (eds). *The Complete Systemic Supervisor: Context, Philosophy, and Pragmatics*. Boston: Allyn and Bacon.

Gendlin, E. T. (1978) *Focusing: How to Gain Direct Access to Your Body's Knowledge: How to Open up Your deeper Feelings and Intuition.* New York: Bantam Dell.

Gendlin, E. T. (2003) *Focusing: How to Gain Direct Access to Your Body's Knowledge: How to Open up Your deeper Feelings and Intuition.* 25th Anniversary Edition. London: Rider.

Gendlin, E. T. (2012) Comment on Thomas Fuchs: the time of the explicating process. In S. C. Koch, T. Fuchs, M. Summa and C. Müller (eds). *Body Memory, Metaphor and Movement.* Amsterdam: John Benjamin's Publishing Company.

Gendlin, E. T. and Heuman, L. (2011) Focusing: an interview with Eugene Gendlin. *Tricycle Magazine*. www.tricycle.com (Fall 2011). Accessed 6 September 2011.

Hernández, P. and McDowell, T. (2010) Intersectionality, power and relational safety in context: key concepts in clinical supervision. *Training and Education in Professional Psychology*, 4(1), 29–35.

Hernández-Wolfe, P. (2010) Family counseling supervision. In N. Ladany and L. Bradely (eds). *Counselor Supervision*. London: Routledge.

Lowe, R. (2005) Structured methods and striking moments: using question sequences in 'living' ways. *Family Process*, 44(1), 65–76.

Maturana, H. and Varela, F. (1980) *Autopoiesis and Cognition: The Realization of the Living*. London: Reidel.

Pearce, W. B. and Pearce, K. A. (1998) Transcendent storytelling: abilities for systemic practitioners and their clients. *Human Systems: The Journal of Systemic Consultation and Management*, 9, 167–85.

Pearce, W. B. (2007) *Making Social Worlds: A Communication Perspective*. Oxford: Blackwell.

Riikonen, E. (1999) Inspiring dialogues and relational responsibility. In S. McNamee and K. J. Gergen (eds). *Relational Responsibility: Resources for Sustainable Dialogue*. London: Sage.

Shotter, J. (2010) *Social Construction on the Edge: 'Withness'– Thinking and Embodiment*. Ohio: Taos Institute Publications.

Shotter, J. and Katz, A. M. (1999) Creating relational realities. Responsible responding to poetic 'movements' and 'moments'. In S. McNamee and K.J. Gergen (eds). *Relational Responsibility: Resources for Sustainable Dialogue*. London: Sage.

Wittgenstein, L. (1953) *Philosophical Investigations*. Oxford: Basil Blackwell.

White, M. (2004) *Narrative Practice and Exotic Lives: Resurrecting Diversity in Everyday Life*. Adelaide, Australia: Dulwich Centre Publications.

8 Bodies in conversation

An approach to body-focused supervision

Jo Bownas

This chapter is about a practice I refer to as body-focused supervision. I will describe how the practice began for me, how I have thought about it and how it has developed. For those who would like to work with these ideas in their own supervision, I offer a practice 'guide': suggested steps in this approach to inviting our bodies into conversation in supervision. My own theoretical orientation in my work is systemic, a relational approach to therapy which often involves working with more than one person 'in the room', attending to patterns of communication and to the multiple layers of personal and societal context that shape our lives. I am influenced by social constructionist understandings of the world, and our experience within it, not as fixed 'found things' but as constructions that constantly evolve in language between people in social interaction. I am also drawn to narrative practices, in which we think of ourselves as constituted by the stories we tell and the stories that are told about our lives and identities. These approaches take account of relationships of power and of how dominant societal discourses shape individual experience. My own orientation and theoretical preferences will be visible in the supervision practice I introduce in this chapter, but the practice evolved somewhat at the margins of what was familiar to me and later found connections with my preferred theoretical language as well as drawing on texts that were new to me. I invite you, the reader, to engage in a similar process: to encounter the practice I offer, being open to resonances with your own experience, making connections with your own preferred theoretical language, and feeling free to discard or develop aspects of the practice in whatever way is useful to you. The practice evolved for me in the context of supervision of systemic therapy, but I think it has applications in supervision of any professional practice that has to do with human encounters.

Introducing myself

I am a systemic psychotherapist and supervisor working with adults and adolescents in a forensic mental health service in London and in private therapy and supervision practice. Since this book is all about 'embodiment', let me not be a disembodied voice as I write. So, to bring my body to the page: I am a short, White woman whose face and form are shaped and inscribed with the experiences of over 50 years of life. If you were to hear me speak you would guess at my English heritage and possibly detect the traces of a 'northern' English accent, faded after 30 years of living in London. As I sit at my desk typing, my legs are crossed and tightly coiled around each other below the knee. My shoulders are slightly hunched. From time to time I look up over my glasses and let my eyes focus on a more distant point, to rest my eyes and to let my gaze turn inwards to memory, thought and sensation. Eventually, my body will protest at my writing posture and I will move, stretch and maybe take a walk. I will be reminded that, although this 'writing' seems to be an activity of the mind, my body is intimately involved and, just as my mental activity 'moves' my body, so my body influences my thoughts and emotions.

Attending to the body

This attention to what my body is doing as I write is not irrelevant, since it returns me to one of the experiences that generated my interest in embodiment in therapy and supervision. A few years ago I injured my back. The pain could be very absorbing and distracting but I discovered that it would more or less go if I sat very still and upright in a high-backed chair. In this posture, I was able to work, giving my full attention to the people with whom I was meeting. But I began to notice that something seemed different in my therapy and supervision sessions: conversations seemed rather stiff and lifeless, I found it hard to make a connection with the people with whom I was talking. After a while, I started to tell people at the start of a session that I would be sitting very still because of my back injury and this may make things seem quite odd, but I was still able to give them my full attention. Giving a narrative to my stillness seemed to help, but I was very glad when my back recovered and I could move freely again. This experience made me reflect on the contribution my body made to therapeutic and supervisory conversations: all the small and large movements, of which I was mostly unaware, that were themselves expressions and responses in the flow of conversation. As Andersen (1998: 75) says, 'language comprises all kinds of utterances. This includes words . . . and bodily activities.' I began to think about how, in the exchange of spoken language, my body and the bodies of those with whom I was speaking were responding to, and with, the words we heard and spoke, and how these 'bodily activities' might be considered part of our conversation.

These events occurred while I was undertaking systemic supervision training and my experience with my own body resonated with questions that were arising for me about how we might attend to and speak about embodied experience in therapy training and supervision. When I began to explore this question in a number of ways for my Supervision MA dissertation, it occurred to me that one setting for my enquiry would be my own supervision, with Glenda Fredman.

Body-focused supervision: a beginning

I took to my own supervision an episode from my practice, foregrounding my bodily experience, and asked Glenda if we could focus on this bodily experience to help with my exploration for my dissertation; I would later reflect on the process and practices of the supervision. As we embarked on this supervision we had no template to work from, but what emerged was a rich experience which, on later reflection, suggested practices that could be repeated. I am hugely indebted to Glenda for her immediate agreement to my request and for the spontaneous wisdom she brought to the encounter.

In my role as a family therapist in a secure hospital, I work with men and women who have committed acts of violence, often while experiencing psychosis. Sometimes these acts of violence are towards family members. The rupture and disorientation that can occur in family relationships when one member violently breaches the boundaries of another's body seem to me distinctive and, in these circumstances, I have often been more than usually aware of the physical presence of participants in family therapy and of the visceral responses of my own body. In this episode of supervision, I brought a story of a recent experience. Firstly, I told my story while Glenda listened. The story, abbreviated, was as follows:

> I had been working for some time with a family who had experienced considerable trauma from a violent attack by a family member (Prudence) who was now a patient in our hospital. Some family members wanted to meet with Prudence. I had been carefully preparing for this meeting for some time, together with Prudence, her clinical team and the family. The evening before the meeting was due to take place, I was at home writing a service report that I had been asked to produce at short notice for a management meeting that was to take place later on the same day as Prudence's family meeting. As I wrote, I was suddenly overcome by an intense feeling of nausea and faintness. I dropped my pen and went to the window, flinging it wide open to breathe the air. I knew with absolute certainty I could not return to writing; I put my papers away without a further thought and went to bed. During the night, I woke feeling feverish, nauseous and aching. I was convinced that I had flu and spent what seemed like hours, battling in the dark, pleading with my body, my God or whoever was listening, to just let me be alright in the morning so that the carefully and anxiously prepared meeting would not be cancelled. At the same time, I worried that if I did go to the family meeting I might give everyone flu. The next morning I woke feeling tired but not ill. The meeting between Prudence and her family went ahead, and I did not develop flu.

Following a different thread: listening with the body

After I had finished speaking, Glenda said that my invitation to tune into body talk had led her to foreground attention to my body as I spoke: she had noticed changes in the tone and pitch of my voice, how my hand moved to press against my chest. She spoke of how, as she intentionally concentrated on my body, my words had receded for her. At times she felt she had 'lost the thread', but realised this was not so, she was just following *a different* thread.

> Words are not only heard or received but they also move the talker. These movements can be seen and felt by the listener, who in turn is moved. Therefore we touch each other and our selves with our expressions and the words we speak move both ourselves and others to different positions.
>
> (Fredman, 2007: 49)

So, in my supervision session, Glenda was touched by my words and bodily expressions and, as she listened, she was aware not only of what *my* body was showing but also of her own bodily responses to my words and expressions: at times she felt hot and flushed; she felt an enormous sense of relief when I said 'I did not get flu' – a sense that 'something had been survived'.

Glenda suggested we think of my story as a resource. She began to share what had particularly 'struck' her about my story, repeating my words: 'battling in the dark' and other phrases that had particularly affected her. Janine Roberts (1994: 9) writes of how there may be no words to describe some events. She says: 'words may mis-describe the events because they cannot capture the horror of them'. She suggests that in the absence of adequate words it may be particularly important that 'tellers and listeners share both the spoken and the unspoken' (p. 11). Here, it seems that Glenda was able to 'receive' in her body a more intense experience than I could convey in words, and she drew my attention to the words that had been connected, for her, with the most intense sensation. As I heard my words and bodily expressions echoed back to me, I was returned to an earlier memory when my body had experienced something similar. A few years ago I had been taking turns to look after a very sick relative, staying with her for several days at a time. More than once, the night before I was due to go to her, I had felt really ill during the night and had been convinced I was coming down with something. I remembered 'battling in the dark' then too, with a sense of wanting and not wanting: it had seemed that, while in my mind and heart I really wanted to look after my relative, my body had shown me something different, perhaps a dread of what I would face and a wish not to have to face it. Now, in my supervision session, I reflected that that had been true of my meeting with Prudence and her family too: I had wanted and not wanted to do it – I had partly dreaded it. And I wondered now about the 'wanting and not wanting' that Prudence and her family might have experienced. Of course, we had talked about their 'mixed feelings', but now I wondered how those feelings and their intentions might be in conflict – 'in battle', and about how that might be experienced and expressed by the family beyond words.

In my ongoing work with the family, I kept this *wondering* alive and began to pay more attention to the bodily complaints family members sometimes spoke of. Sometimes, of course, a headache is just a headache! But with Prudence's family

I found that connecting with their present experience of a physical discomfort could, at times, allow them to articulate thoughts and feelings that had previously been unspoken.

The body gets ready for action

Griffith and Elliott Griffith (1994: 45) describe an emotion, 'in a biological sense' as 'a dynamic disposition of the body for action . . .'. They use the term 'emotional posture' to denote how, during a specific emotion, the body is readied for specific action. In therapy, they ask 'if you were to think of your body as getting ready for a particular kind of action or . . . expression, what would that be?' (p. 46) In the episode I brought to supervision, we might say that my body had readied itself, through sickness, to retreat from what I was intending to do, to be too ill to go ahead with the meeting. Griffith and Elliott Griffith go on to 'inquire about which self-narratives are bound to this emotional posture: What are the important parts of life experience tightly connected to this specific emotion?' (p. 114). In my supervision session, I spontaneously recalled an earlier life experience that was 'tightly connected' with my recent embodied response, and this opened a richer narrative for me to move around in, as I thought about my own experience and that of the family I was working with. Turp (1999) writes about 'body storylines', and I think I could refer to the process I have just described as *tracing a body storyline* – a thread of experience that is written on the body.

Following a body storyline

Within this storyline I made another connection with the present: during those nights when I was battling in the dark, before going to look after my relative, my body had given me a real dilemma: if I *did* manage to go to look after her and I *did* have a virus, I could do her harm by giving her my virus. And that had been true of my battle in the dark before Prudence's family meeting too: I had feared that if I did go ahead with the meeting I could give everyone flu. Looking back, I realised I had already been worrying that the planned meeting could do harm as well as potentially doing good, and I knew that at least some members of the family had that fear too. Maybe my body was alerting me to keep myself open to both possibilities, of good and of harm. I resolved to keep listening to that embodied voice in the future work. Thus, in my future meetings with Prudence and her family, I returned to the theme of balancing 'good and harm', checking with different family members regularly where they stood on this continuum *right now.* I found that this made room for considerable variation between family members and with the same family members at different points in time.

Looking inside the words

The supervision session continued and Glenda told me that, as she had listened to my narrative, her body had responded to my use of the word 'nausea'. She offered a story from her own life that connected her with that bodily sensation.

> As a young woman studying in apartheid South Africa Glenda was preparing to attend a demonstration, campaigning for equality for Black students. As she got ready to go to the demonstration she felt overwhelmed by a feeling of nausea. She thought she might not be able to go, but somehow she did.

After telling her story, Glenda suggested we both *look inside* the feeling of nausea (Andersen, 1995). Looking inside, Glenda found 'rage' and 'sadness', and her use of the word 'rage' immediately struck a chord with me. I had been enraged by the demand that I produce a (management) report at such short notice and at such a moment. With 'nausea' my body had prepared me to reject decisively that demand and to give my full attention to what was really important to me. As Leder (1984: 31) proposes, the body is intentional: 'it is the body which first understands the world, grasping its surroundings and moving to fulfil its goals'. My connection with 'rage' also then led me to think more about the place of rage in the story of Prudence and her family. As I returned to working with the family I did not press 'rage' upon them, but my own encounter with it in my body's protest kept me alert to the possibility that it might be part of their narrative too. I looked for openings in our conversations that might allow the family to speak of 'rage and protest' in their own words.

Oppression and what the body knows

Later Glenda's story returned to me and I recalled that it had contained an element of protest against racist oppression. My attention was drawn to how we embody aspects of social difference – my body shows my gender and race, for instance, and of course, power and privilege are associated with those embodied differences. This made me wonder more about what discourses of difference and oppression might be called forth for Prudence, a Black woman of African heritage, and her family in meeting with me, a White woman. I was reminded of bel hooks (1994: 91) who describes 'a way of knowing', particularly arising from suffering associated with oppression, that is often 'expressed through the body, what it knows, what has been deeply inscribed on it through experience'. In the work with the family we had already spoken about the particular meanings that were given to Prudence's actions within the family's cultural community; and the family had brought to my attention the many ways in which the powerful institution of which I was part, embedded in the dominant culture, misread the family's experience and needs. Following my supervision session, however, the family and I began to make more connections between their experience of oppression, in their own country of origin as well as in Britain, and Prudence's attack on the 'body' of her family.

The body's biography

Shaw (2003: 46) writes that therapists (and we could add supervisors) 'bring their own biographical lived-body to the situation and it is by sharing these experiences that an embodied therapeutic narrative can be developed'. This seems to describe well something of what happened in my supervision session: Glenda's story was from her own lived-body biography, and, at a narrative level, it had nothing to do with what I had been talking about, just as the story from my own lived-body biography, of caring for my sick relative, had no direct connection with the story of Prudence's family. But Glenda's story had been stirred in her memory by her bodily resonance with my story and my embodied telling. In turn, aspects of her story resonated with me in ways that were connected with, but separate from, Glenda's. As my story was told and reflected back to me, as Glenda's story and mine intertwined, as my bodily expressions and Glenda's echoed between us and found words, some new meanings and new possibilities emerged. Roberts (1994: 8) suggests there may be 'different levels of telling', with each repeated telling moving the teller to a different position – 'the mind often coheres and connects things it hears being spoken in a new way . . . the same story is never told twice'. By bringing our bodies into the conversation it seemed we had accessed a different 'level of telling', opening up different positions and new connections.

Bodies in conversation

The theoretical connections embedded in the account of my supervision session above were made on later reflection, outside the supervision session, when I asked myself, 'What happened here?' My conversation with Glenda had involved words, some of which referred to bodily sensations, but it also involved an experiencing of bodily sensation in the moment and the linking, in turn, of those sensations with words and stories. John Shotter (2008: 7) refers to 'spontaneous bodily responsiveness' and to 'the enormous grasp of detail available to us in our ways of knowing how to make sense of the myriad events occurring around us, and our embodied ways of spontaneously reacting to them' (p. 12). It seemed that, by intentionally focusing on our bodies in their spontaneous responsiveness, we entertained the possibility that there are 'ways of knowing how to make sense' contained in these responses. In this process Glenda and I had each recovered stories from our own lives that had no apparent connection with the episode I had brought for supervision, but which yielded fresh ways of making sense of and knowing how to go on in my work. Griffiths and Elliott Griffith (1994: 34) argue that 'stories, and not isolated events, are the basic units of human experience'. They suggest that, in the frequent immediacy of our reactions (for example, a man whirls round to confront a potential attacker when the shadow of a tree falls across his path) stories 'appear too quickly and in too much complexity to be constructed de novo out of primitive sensations of the moment . . . the stories must have been already present, drawn from a canon of stories that stand ready to structure how we experience our lived world'. We might say that, in our supervision session, Glenda and I found stories that 'stood ready'; as if, in the river of stories in which we are each immersed, bodily experience and the words that accompanied it acted like a hook, catching one particular story from the river for us to take out and look at.

Shotter (2008: 8) cautions against understanding 'spontaneous bodily responsiveness' as implying that 'there is a "body language" at work unrecognised in the background in the use of our words'. This seems to me an important warning that we cannot 'interpret' the bodily expressions of another or assume a correspondence between our embodied experience, or the stories it generates, and the experience or stories of the other. When Glenda offered me her felt and embodied responses to my story, she did not suggest these were *my* feelings or responses. She offered them as her own and she made space for *my* resonances with *her* responses. The title of this chapter is 'Bodies in conversation' and, for me, it is important in this kind of work to remember that there are two bodies present, two biographical lived-bodies. What happens between us when we open ourselves to our embodied responses is not, I think, a one-way communication from client to therapist or supervisee to supervisor, it is an interactional event. As supervisors, our responses are our own, and connected with our own lived-body biographies. But, by bringing those responses and connections to the supervision table, we may offer our supervisees a fresh narrative landscape in which to wander with curiosity.

Developing the supervision practice

Reflecting on the experience of my supervision session with Glenda, I was able to identify a number of steps or activities of the supervisor that I thought could be developed into a supervision practice that could be repeated:

- Agreeing with the supervisee to engage in an episode of body-focused supervision.
- Listening and tuning in to the supervisee's bodily expression as well as their words.
- Supervisor noticing their own embodied responses as they listen.
- Supervisor sharing their own responses and inviting the supervisee to respond to their responses.
- Inviting and sharing connections with stories from the lived biographies of supervisee and/or supervisor.
- Exploring these stories for possible connections with the work brought to supervision.

These steps are elaborated in the supervisors' guide (pp. 115–17).

I have gone on to use this practice in my own work as a supervisor and I have also used the supervisors' guide in training and workshops. In practice, I do not necessarily follow the steps in sequence or start a supervision session with the intention that it will be 'body-focused'. Rather I hold these practices as possibilities among a repertoire of possibilities that I can offer to the supervisee if it seems they might be helpful. What follows is an example of how body-focused practice may be woven into a supervision session.

Body-focused supervision and the boy who would not slow down

In supervision, Naomi, a family therapist, spoke of an episode involving a family session with a young teenager, Jon, who was in temporary foster care since relationships had 'broken down' at home.

> The family session took place in the child and adolescent mental health service (CAMHS) clinic local to the family home. It was agreed Naomi would accompany Jon to and from the session. The session with the family had gone well, but Naomi wanted to address her concerns about the return journey from the clinic with Jon. She and Jon travelled by bus and there was quite a long walk between the bus stop and the CAMHS clinic. On the way there Naomi discovered that Jon was a 'fast walker and [she] struggled to keep up with him'. On the return journey she 'just could not keep up with him at all'. She repeatedly called out to Jon to slow down and wait for her but in the end, 'physically incapable of walking any faster, (she) gave up and stopped trying', resigning herself to 'losing' him. Naomi spoke very fast as she gave this account and her description in words was accompanied by expressions of her body conveying intense effort followed by exhaustion. In my own body I felt a breathless urgency as I listened to her. She told me she had felt very 'anxious' about 'failing' in her 'responsibility' to return Jon safely to his foster home and very relieved when Jon eventually slowed down and returned to join her. She wanted to reflect on her responsibilities in this kind of situation and also on possible understandings of Jon's behaviour – which he had been unable to give words to at the time, despite Naomi's enquiries.

In supervision we explored Naomi's concern about the possibility of 'failing' to return Jon to his foster home, and about how future visits to the clinic might be negotiated and planned. We also thought about how we might understand Jon's actions in walking so far ahead of Naomi. Did he want to 'hurry away' from his family session? Did he not want to be seen in his home neighbourhood with a strange woman? Was he enjoying his physical ability, superior to Naomi's? Or was he simply not aware of the distance he was creating between himself and Naomi, leaving the job of 'coordinating' to her until he realised she was not there, at which point he returned to look for her? I was aware of the embodied nature of the episode that Naomi had described and the way I had experienced her account in my own body. So I asked Naomi if, since this seemed to have been a very physical encounter, she would be interested in exploring the episode from a bodily perspective, to see if this had anything to offer us.

Naomi agreed and I shared with her my own bodily experience as I had listened to her: a feeling of 'breathlessness' and 'anxious urgency'. I said I had been particularly struck by her expression 'physically incapable'. Naomi responded by describing more fully how she had 'strained every muscle' to keep up with Jon, how she had felt 'breathless, hot and panicky' until it had come to her that she 'just could not do it', that her 'legs could not go any faster'. Then she stopped for a moment, resumed walking at her own natural pace and quickly felt a sense of 'physical relief' that she was not forcing herself to try any more. At the same time, she felt 'defeated', that she had 'failed', and she was aware of feeling 'angry' with Jon for not heeding her cries to slow down. After listening to Naomi, I said I was powerfully drawn to her words 'just could not do it', the sense that she had pushed her body to its limit, but 'just could not do it'. I wondered if there was a story from our own life narratives that might connect us with this experience. We both thought for a moment and then I offered a story from my lived-body biography:

> In my secondary school we had singing lessons once a week. During the class, the teacher would pick a row of pupils who would be asked to stand up one at a time and sing three notes: 'doh, re, doh'. A simple exercise, but one I was completely incapable of performing. I could hear that I was not hitting the note and I wanted to with every fibre of my being – but I just could not make my body do it. The teacher could not accept that I could not do it and would make me repeat the exercise over and over. Along the way I gave up trying, just going through the motions of the exercise and resigning myself to feelings of frustration with my body, humiliation in front of my classmates and anger towards the teacher for exposing my failure.

Naomi's response to my story was to express compassion for my young self, and she reflected about how she might feel compassion for herself in the situation she had described with Jon. We went on to consider whether our stories might have anything to offer us as a resource for thinking about the work with Jon. Naomi said she thought there was a strong connection. My story had brought to mind how Jon had experienced many distressing events in his life and his schooling had been much disrupted. He was identified as having difficulties in learning and struggled particularly with language. Drawing on our stories, Naomi wondered whether Jon experienced that sensation of 'just can't do it', no matter how much he tried; whether he also felt defeated, humiliated and angry with those who persistently exposed his limitations and 'lost' him as they marched ahead in language, expecting him to follow when he could not. Naomi wondered whether these feelings could be present for Jon at times when he appeared sullenly silent in her (language-based) sessions with him and his family, or at times when he appeared aggressively defiant in his life. Together we thought about what Naomi's work with Jon would look like if she brought to it the compassion she had experienced in relation to my story. Naomi recalled the relief she had felt when Jon returned to where *she* was on their journey and the pleasure of having him walk with her for a while at her pace. She began to think of how she and others could be with Jon at *his* pace, working with him in ways that engaged his physical and artistic abilities rather than dragging him behind in (for him) an impossibly fast march of language.

In our supervision session we had already discussed ideas that seemed to help Naomi make sense of her experience and think about her future work with Jon. When we brought our bodies into the conversation we did not necessarily have 'better' or 'truer' ideas, but we did find ourselves in a new narrative landscape, with opportunities for exploration of fresh territory and a sense of the rich potential of an embodied 'knowing' in the work with Jon.

Introducing the guide

Following is a guide for supervisors who might like to try using body-focused supervision. The guide offers a step-by-step approach. You may find it useful to follow each step in turn while you are exploring and familiarising yourself with the practice. It is necessary to include the step *Listening, resonating, responding*. Later, you may choose to use or adapt stages of the practice that fit best with your own approach to supervision or that suggest themselves as having more potential in a particular episode of supervision.

It is important to remind ourselves that our bodies and their expressions can be held as very private, and drawing attention to them without invitation may be experienced as intrusive. Body-focused supervision, as I have proposed it in this chapter, is intended as a collaborative practice, between supervisor and supervisee, with the implicit expectation that both openly consent to bringing their bodies to the supervision conversation.

Guide 8.1 An approach to body-focused supervision

Invite the supervisee to tell the story of the issue she or he is bringing to supervision.

Listening, resonating, responding

- While the supervisee is telling the story, pay attention to the words and bodily activities of the teller (e.g. facial expression, gesture, breathing, tone of voice).
- As you listen, your intention is to be open to resonances with the supervisee's experience, as expressed *in* words and *beyond* words.
  - Notice any words or phrases that strike you, touch you, move you.
  - Notice what your own body is doing, your physical or emotional sensations.

Don't worry if you lose the thread of the story; just notice what draws your attention.

- When the supervisee has finished telling her/his story, share your experience and responses during listening. Reflect on:
  - their words, phrases or bodily activities that struck you
  - the physical or emotional sensations you noticed in yourself as you listened.
- Enquire: *'As you listened to me did anything draw your attention/stand out for you in my responses?'*
  - *'Do you make any connections with your story?'*

Focusing on the supervisee's responses

- Attend to a part of the supervisee's story in which s/he described an emotion or bodily sensation and enquire:
  - *'If you were to think of your body as getting ready for a particular kind of action or expression, what would that be?'*
  - *'How might that action or expression relate to the episode you described?'*
  - *'What parts of your life experience are closely connected to this emotion or bodily sensation?'*
  - *'Is there a story from your life that occurs to you now?'*

(The supervisee may wish to tell the story or just to think about it quietly.)

- Enquire: *'If we think of this story from your self-narrative as a resource, does it have anything to offer you in relation to the episode you recounted earlier?'*

Focusing on the supervisor's responses

- Attend to a word or phrase from the supervisee's story that struck you (supervisor), perhaps one that evoked a strong physical or emotional response in you as you listened.
- Look inside that word, phrase or embodied response and describe what you see: is there a story from your (supervisor's) own self-narrative that connects you with that word, phrase or bodily sensation?
  (If you feel comfortable, share that story with your supervisee.)
- Enquire: *'If we think of my story as a resource, is there anything that struck you as you listened?'*
  - *'Does my story have anything to offer you in relation to the episode you recounted earlier?'*

Gathering possibilities

- Invite the supervisee to reflect on what has emerged between you:
  - *'Have any new ideas been generated?'*
  - *'How might you (supervisee) take these ideas forward into your work?'* (Remembering these are just *ideas* and not truths about the people the supervisee is working with.)

References

Andersen, T. (1995) Reflecting processes; acts of informing and forming: you can borrow my eyes but you must not take them away from me! In S. Friedman (ed.). *The Reflecting Team in Action: Collaborative Practice in Family Therapy.* New York: Guilford.

Andersen, T. (1998) One sentence of five lines about creating meaning. *Human Systems: The Journal of Systemic Consultation and Management*, 9(2), 73–80.

Fredman, G. (2007) Preparing ourselves for the therapeutic relationship. *Human Systems: The Journal of Systemic Consultation and Management*, 18, 44–59.

Griffith, J. L. and Elliott Griffith, M. (1994) *The Body Speaks. Therapeutic Dialogues for Mind–Body Problems*. New York: Basic Books.

hooks, b. (1994) *Teaching to Transgress: Education as the Practice of Freedom.* London: Routledge.

Leder, D. (1984) Medicine and paradigms of embodiment. *The Journal of Medicine and Philosophy*, 4, 29–43

Roberts, J. (1994) *Tales and Transformations.* New York: W. W. Norton and Company.

Shaw, R. (2003) *The Embodied Psychotherapist: The Therapist's Body Story.* London & New York: Routledge.

Shotter, J. (2008) *Conversational Realities Revisited: Life, Language, Body and World.* Chagrin Falls, OH: Taos Institute.

Turp, M. (1999) Working with body storylines. *Psychodynamic Counselling*, 5(3), 301–17.

9 Supervision of arousal and disgust

Catherine Butler and Glenda Fredman

We are writing this chapter in the contexts of our work as systemic psychotherapists, supervisors and supervisees, drawing on our practice as clinical psychologists in sexual health and child and adolescent medicine services within our public health service. This work often involves conversations with clients, supervisees and supervisors about intimate bodily experiences, including sexual feelings and behaviour that can challenge our usual professional psychotherapy discourses. In supervision with us, supervisees from a range of services have presented both arousal and disgust as unwanted bodily sensations in relation to clients and have described difficulty 'admitting' these feelings to themselves or supervisors. This chapter focuses on supervision practices we have developed to address strong bodily sensations and experiences of arousal and disgust in supervision conversations.

I (Catherine) first addressed therapist arousal and disgust in a keynote speech at a British Association of Sex and Relationship Therapists (BASRT) conference (Butler, 2010) with a view to breaking the potential taboo of talking about these bodily sensations in relation to therapy. I had chosen this topic as I had never heard this issue openly discussed amongst therapists. Raising it as a supervisor or supervisee felt challenging. Breaking this taboo resulted in many people I had never met approaching me that evening at the conference social, to tell me about their feelings of arousal and disgust that arose in, and sometimes lingered after, therapy. In this chapter, we build upon those early ideas (Butler, 2011) and connect them to supervision practice.

Pope and Tabachnick (1993) found that therapists in adult services reported a range of feelings in relation to clients, including anger, hate, fear and sexual feelings. Fifty-eight per cent of therapists they surveyed reported a time when they had felt physical sexual arousal in a client's presence. Sexual arousal could be triggered for a range of reasons, not just as a direct result of the client or supervisee or the material under discussion. For example, discussing a client's sex life could trigger unbidden personal memories of sex and related bodily sensations.

Talking about arousal and disgust

Although Marzillier (2010: 234) tells us it is 'no surprise that psychotherapists become sexually attracted to their patients [since] theirs is a relationship of intimacy' and Yalom (2010) matter-of-factly addresses how therapists can manage their feelings of revulsion towards their clients, therapists' feelings of arousal and disgust are still a taboo subject. Pope and Tabachnick (1993) note that it is quite common for therapists, like Jacob (below), to find it extremely difficult to acknowledge to themselves that they experience these feelings in clinical work.

Blushing with excitement

> Jacob, a White male supervisee of a similar age to me (Catherine) and also a clinical psychologist, told me in supervision that he was 'embarrassed to admit' feeling 'attracted' to a female client, Leanne, with whom he was meeting to address her 'social anxiety', which had left her feeling 'lonely'. When I asked how he was experiencing this 'attraction' (with questions like 'How do you know this is attraction?', 'Is it something you feel/think?', 'How does it affect you?'), Jacob disclosed that he felt 'excited' before Leanne's session and found himself having to 'look away' and 'control my humour' in case he 'came across as flirting'. Jacob feared that he blushed when 'I caught myself thinking that I would like to ask her out . . . could have a relationship with her if I met her socially . . . if she was not my client'. I noticed Jacob blush as he spoke.

Pope *et al.* (2005) found that therapists rarely talked about arousal and disgust in supervision. Supervisees feared that the supervisor may misunderstand them, take what they said out of context or even misuse their disclosure. John Marzillier (2010: 234), in his memoirs of his life as a psychotherapist, describes feeling sexually attracted to a female patient to whom he was teaching relaxation. 'In my mind's eye I undressed her and fantasised frantic coupling as we fell into each other's arms'. This experience shocked him and made him pause, but 'there was no one to talk to about it for in my behaviour therapy days, relationships were not what mattered'.

Before we even begin talking about unwanted feelings like arousal or disgust in supervision, we spend time warming the context (Burnham, 2005) for this kind of talk by 'talking about talking' (Fredman, 1997) with supervisees.

Talking about talking

Although we find that transparently discussing the dilemmas posed by feelings of arousal or disgust can open space for learning and contribute to safe practice, we do not make the assumption that supervisees should talk or that they want to talk with *us* about their feelings in supervision. Fredman (2004: 12) cites several examples where practitioners assert they would not expect to discuss feelings at work at all, and therefore 'put feelings aside and get on with the job' or even 'take feelings off and hang them on the hook with the coats at the start of each shift', lest talking about the feelings might 'interfere with focusing on the task in hand'.

Therefore we always begin with questions to ourselves, as supervisors, to consider whether we have a suitable context for talking (Fredman, 1997). We go on to check with supervisees whether we have created the kind of relationship that can enable a useful conversation in which the supervisee feels respected and understood.

> Thus, I (Catherine) asked Jacob 'Would it feel Ok for us to talk a bit more about this?' and checked from time to time, 'How is this talking going? What is it like discussing this with me?' I learned that Jacob felt 'comfortable' talking with me since previous informal discussions between us in the workplace about his 'looking for a relationship' seemed to warm the context for him to bring this to supervision.

Sometimes, when supervising, we directly raise the challenge of broaching feelings of arousal or disgust in supervision, acknowledging that experiencing arousal or disgust in relation to clients might feel less acceptable to us, as therapists, than other feelings like joy, sadness or anger. We explore supervisees' *views on talking* about these feelings and experiences (*'What are your views on talking about [arousal/disgust] with me?'*) and what *kinds of talking* they consider useful, wanted and not wanted (*'Are there some things you do not want to talk about here with me?' 'How would I know we are talking in ways you do/do not want?'*). This includes inviting supervisees to anticipate the *effects of talking* about arousal and disgust on themselves, their relationship with clients and on our supervisory relationship.

> After describing how he felt about the client, Jacob went on to explain that these feelings of 'attraction' towards his client were unusual for him to experience in therapy and so left him feeling 'deskilled' and 'unprofessional' adding, 'And I'm worried that you might think I am unprofessional too.'

Talking in different domains

Supervisors do, of course, have responsibilities in what Lang *et al.* (1990) call the *domain of production* for ensuring that the supervisee maintains safe, ethical and effective practice: responsibilities that might include monitoring risk or implementing legal, professional or service policies. Christine Oliver (2005) suggests that when managers talk in the *domain of production* the intention is evaluative, when talking in the *domain of explanation* they adopt a facilitative intent and in the *aesthetic domain* conversation is reflexive. Sharon Bond (chapter 4) reviews these Domains of Action in relation to supervision and includes a *domain of rhetoric*.

We try to meet supervision responsibilities for ensuring ethical and competent practice aesthetically by open and collaborative dialogue with supervisees, appreciating the supervisees' professionalism when they bring their concerns to supervision. Therefore we usually start with evaluating together whether any action is needed to ensure safety and effectiveness, exploring, for example, whether the supervisee is asking for permission to withdraw from this therapy because of overwhelming feelings of arousal or disgust.

As with many dilemmas brought to supervision, it may sometimes be helpful to talk explicitly in the *domain of production* for a while before deciding together that no practical action is needed and the conversation can enter the exploratory mode of the *domain of explanation*. Similarly, the conversation may begin in the *domain of explanation* but, in the course of facilitative exploration, the supervisor may become aware that some practical action may be needed and may then suggest to the supervisee that they move into *domain of production* talk for a while. Again, talking in this domain need not involve 'judgement' or 'investigation' of the supervisee by the supervisor, but can be a collaborative evaluation of the situation by supervisee and supervisor leading to joint decisions about any practical action needed.

When supervisees disclose strong feelings of arousal or disgust, we usually begin exploring their own evaluation of the feeling in the *domain of explanation* and *aesthetics*. We ask ourselves, 'Does it feel comfortable and safe to remain in the *domain of explanation* and/or aesthetics to unpack these feelings of arousal or disgust?' We notice when and if we feel a pull into the *domain of production* to investigate the therapist's professionalism. During the conversation with Jacob, Catherine moved aesthetically between the *domain of explanation* (exploring how he felt about his arousal and how he understood this in relation to his professionalism) and the *domain of production* (addressing what Jacob did about these feelings in the work) holding the professional code of conduct as the highest context.

Core and moral disgust in supervision

A baby toe in a bucket of blood

> A nurse asked me (Glenda), a paediatric psychologist, to join her while she bathed a little boy's foot. He had a rare disease which caused his skin and nails to blister and thicken, requiring constant dressing changes and careful bathing that was always excruciatingly painful. I often supported nurses and children with 'pain management' during these sorts of procedures and the nurse was hoping I could help alleviate some of the boy's distress. As the nurse patiently and sensitively bathed the boy's foot, I witnessed his baby toe fall off in a bucket of blood. I felt sick and wanted to retch. I fought to control my face from expressing the disgust I was feeling, trying desperately to counter my tightening facial muscles, while the little boy screamed in pain. Afterwards I worried that the boy had witnessed my expression of disgust. I beat myself up in supervision, believing I should model myself on the nurse who managed to control herself to the point, I imagined, she did not even feel anything but compassion.

De Jong *et al.* (2010) distinguish between 'core disgust' and 'social–moral disgust'. They suggest that core disgust is an inbuilt evolutionary process to distance oneself from environmental pathogens, such as vomit or faeces. *Core disgust* has physiological origins and is first experienced as a spontaneous bodily response that may lead to moral judgements. We might describe Glenda's initial response to the foul smell of pus and the sight of a small toe floating in blood and skin as *core disgust. Social–moral disgust*, on the other hand, appears to originate in a moral position when a culture's socio-moral rules are transgressed. *Social–moral disgust* may lead on to a bodily experience of 'disgust' as Tamar describes in the following example.

This felt so wrong . . . disgusting . . . and then I felt sick to my stomach

> In supervision with me (Catherine), a trainee psychotherapist, Tamar, said she was finding her client, Lisa, 'difficult to work with' because she 'could not stop myself feeling disgusted and angry'. Tamar explained that she was 'put off' and 'appalled' when Lisa described in detail her experience of human branding. She winced and grimaced as she recounted Lisa's story, 'She actually chose to do this to decorate her body. I had to sit through her detailed description of how the brander used a one-inch bar of metal, kept heating it, putting it against her skin and burning a zig-zag pattern right across her stomach below her bellybutton. She was so graphic, describing how her body started to shake as the bar got nearer and she felt its heat before actual contact. She even described the smell of burning "like cooking meat" each time the red hot bar touched her skin. I could not think in the session. It wasn't so much the gory details – actually that did not bother me that much. I just could not listen to her – I don't know . . . this felt so wrong. And I kept thinking, "You should not be doing this to yourself – it is disgusting" – and then I felt sick to my stomach.'

Thus, Tamar describes first experiencing a moral judgement ('*this felt so wrong*') which she names as 'disgust', and it seems that it is this moral position that then evokes a response in her body ('*I felt sick to my stomach*').

Everyone experiences disgust and arousal. Psycho-biology teaches us that adrenaline can produce bodily responses which might be interpreted as anxiety, arousal or disgust, depending on the meaning assigned to them by the person experiencing them. Arousal and disgust may be felt independent of each other, or at the same time (thus, perhaps leaving one feeling disturbed by being aroused by something one also finds disgusting). As with social–moral disgust, arousal can involve our moral order whereby practitioners, like Jacob and Glenda, assign moral meanings to their bodily experience and thus express difficulty 'confessing' or 'admitting' their experiences of arousal and disgust in supervision, because of fear of judgement from the supervisor, or self-doubt about whether they are 'practising professionally' when experiencing these unwanted feelings.

Like Tamar, we have noticed that feelings of arousal or disgust can close down conversations and create distance and judgement within both the therapeutic and supervisory relationship. Therefore, we find it useful, as supervisors, to begin by exploring our relationship to disclosure of arousal and disgust.

Exploring our relationship to disclosure of arousal and disgust in supervision

We invite you, our reader, to reflect on some of the questions we ask ourselves and supervisees, to consider our relationship to disclosure of arousal and disgust. We invite you to start by re-reading the account of 'arousal' expressed by Jacob or one of the accounts of 'disgust' shared by Glenda or Tamar. Or perhaps, you prefer to choose an example from your own practice. You might like to position yourself in two different ways:

1 First tuning into your own bodily response to the account with questions like: *'What feeling do you have now?' 'Describe the feeling. Where or how do you experience it?' 'How does it affect you?' 'How does it show on/through your body?' 'Is it a positive or negative feeling to feel this way?' 'Where do you get your ideas about this feeling from?'*
2 You might then like to position yourself as a supervisor to Jacob or Glenda and consider your response to the supervisee's expression (of arousal or disgust) with questions like: *'How has the supervisee's disclosure (of arousal/disgust) affected your curiosity about the supervisee's situation?' 'Has your curiosity been inspired or stifled?' 'What are you more/less curious about?' 'How might you view a therapist who brought these feelings to supervision?' 'How might this disclosure influence your view of the therapist's competence/professionalism (positively and negatively)?' 'What informs your ideas? Where do your ideas come from?'*

When we have worked with these sorts of questions in training or supervision, practitioners have shared their own feelings of arousal or disgust in their professional lives and their experiences of talking about these feelings with supervisees and supervisors. Many supervisors described examples where the supervisee's accounts had evoked strong feelings for themselves. When their own strong feelings of arousal and disgust were evoked, they found it harder to 'stay with' the supervisee's experience or dilemma since they were 'trying to manage' or were being 'distracted by' their own feelings, which interfered with their curiosity about the supervisee's or client's situation.

Pope *et al.* (2005) suggest that admitting feelings of arousal and disgust is counter to notions practitioners may hold of being a caring empathic professional, there to help those in need. Therefore practitioners, like Jacob, make negative judgements about those feelings, or may even feel ashamed of them, as Glenda describes in relation to disgust. Most practitioners to whom we have presented these examples, described Jacob and Glenda, in those vignettes, as 'brave', 'ethical' or 'reflexive' in their disclosure of their feelings of arousal and disgust in supervision. However, like Jacob and Glenda, they too would evaluate *themselves* negatively for experiencing or showing similar feelings in a therapy or supervision context. Many practitioners were unsure they would disclose such strong personal responses in their own supervision unless they were 'confident my own supervisor will hold onto multiple perspectives . . . hear my dilemmas . . . not be quick to judge me'. However, they 'hoped' and 'expected' that their own supervisees would 'feel able to bring these sorts of feelings to supervision'.

What the practitioner and supervisor make of their own and others' bodily sensations and whether they deem it appropriate to disclose or talk about them in supervision, will be informed by their socio-cultural understanding of these experiences and the meanings made within the contexts of their culture, family, training, relationship, self-story and the episode in which it occurs (Pearce and Cronen, 1980). Thus, arousal and disgust involve judgement.

Arousal and disgust involve judgement

We ascribe value and meaning to feelings of disgust and arousal such as whether they are desirable or unwanted, suitable or unsuitable, positive or negative. We also make judgements about whether and how the feeling should be expressed. There are always stories connected to our judgements. These stories are generated and informed through our cultures and they inform the stories we tell of our selves and our identities (Fredman, 2004).

The judgements we make about our emotions inform rules, often unspoken, that govern our expression of feeling. We continue to form these rules from an early age as we learn to *do* emotions in our cultures. These rules guide our actions including whether and how we show and perform the emotions. Therefore, we learn what emotions are acceptable, permissible, forbidden, obligatory or questionable to feel, express, do, think and name. Jacob was embarrassed to feel 'attraction' and to be 'excited' by a female client and judged himself as 'unprofessional' and possibly less skilled for feeling aroused. Glenda, too, judged herself negatively, 'beat [herself] up' believing she 'should' control herself like the nurse and 'not feel anything but compassion'. Therefore, when exploring arousal and disgust with people in supervision, we consider the following: 'What judgement is being expressed by, or made about, this feeling/disclosure of arousal/disgust?' And since there are always stories connected with the judgements: 'What stories are connected with this feeling/disclosure of arousal/disgust?' We tune in to words people use to express their moral orders (Cronen and Pearce, 1994) like 'must/must not', 'can/cannot', 'should/should not', and may explore what affordances or constraints these rules create with questions like 'How does holding that rule help you/the client?' 'What difficulties obstacles does it create for you/others?'

Exploring contexts informing our stories and judgements

The stories that inform how we judge or evaluate our feelings and expressions are not created in isolation. We construct these stories in relationship with others, present or absent, including our families and communities. Several different contexts might inform the stories we create, the meanings we develop and the actions we take regarding our experiences. As well as the time, place and relationships of the immediate therapy or supervision situation, these contexts include the cultures of our ethnicity, family, community, gender, age, religion, profession and sexuality. So we explore with people the contexts of their judgements with questions like: *'Where does that (judgement or idea) come from?' 'Whose voices do you hear (telling that rule)?' 'What do they say (that can open space for a story to be told)?'* (Fredman, 2004).

Informed by the cultural rules of his family, gender, sexuality and age group/generation, Jacob was clear that 'of course it is normal to feel aroused by a sexual partner . . . or by an attractive woman in a social situation'. However, according to his professional rules, he was certain that 'I could never have sex with a client' and further extrapolated that he 'should never feel aroused' in the presence of a client. Jacob shared stories from his profession of 'psychologists who have been struck off' for having sexual relationships with clients. This rule and the connected stories seemed to afford a 'sort of protection', helping Jacob to maintain professional boundaries. But they also constrained him from acknowledging his normal spontaneous bodily responses to the extent that he questioned his competence and had a negative view of himself as unethical and unprofessional. By deconstructing Jacob's judgements and rules in supervision, Jacob and I (Catherine) were able to generate a more helpful rule that, 'should we experience arousal in therapy, we may accept the feeling without negatively judging ourselves; but never act on it in relation to clients'.

We invite you, our reader, to explore your contexts, stories and rules in relation to feeling and expressing arousal and disgust with an exercise (see Exercise 9.1 on p. 126). You may choose to practise this exercise in peer supervision with colleagues or share it with a supervision group.

The questions in Exercise 9.1 informed Catherine's conversation with Tamar in supervision.

Exploring strong feelings of arousal and disgust in supervision

Tamar and I (Catherine) briefly 'talked about talking' about the 'disgust' she had expressed and named in response to her client, Lisa's, account of human branding. Tamar welcomed this sort of talk with me, hoping it might help her 'be more present' with Lisa and 'not judge' her. Therefore I went on to introduce the idea of 'moral orders' (Cronen and Lang, 1994) to Tamar, explaining that 'We can sometimes feel strong feelings when our own ideas of right and wrong are being stepped on.' I checked, 'Is it OK for you to feel disgusted in that way with Lisa?'

TAMAR: No – not at all. I felt really bad about it because I **shouldn't judge** her. She has made her own decision. She has not come for help with branding. She is not asking my opinion about it. It's **not for me to judge** . . . **she needs to feel respected** by me . . . otherwise . . . .

CATHERINE: And where does this idea come from – that . . .

TAMAR: **I need to focus on engaging** her so we have a strong therapeutic alliance.

By paying to attention to Tamar's words like 'must/must not', 'can cannot', 'should/should not', 'need to' as moral indicators of what she believed was obligatory, forbidden, expected and permissible, I (Catherine) was able to notice her making several judgements (**in bold**, above). When I explored, 'Whose voices do you hear telling you that you should focus on the therapeutic alliance? Who agrees?' Tamar cited psychotherapy research and the code of ethics and professional conduct of her profession that instructed her to 'always treat clients with respect . . . respect clients' autonomy . . . not allow my prejudice about their lifestyle to adversely affect the way I relate to clients'.

Exercise 9.1 Exploring contexts, stories and rules of arousal and disgust

Starting with a personal exercise:

- Think of a client you work with where you felt aroused/sexually excited or experienced revulsion/felt disgusted.
- Identify a specific episode in your meetings with this client when you experienced or showed these feelings [of arousal/disgust].
- Ask yourself the question: Is it OK to have/express this feeling [of arousal/disgust] with this client here?

Reflect on the rules and stories connected to the judgements you have made: If you are doing this exercise on your own, you may like to make some notes. If you are working with others, you could interview each other using these questions to reflect on:

- What sorts of **judgements** are you making?
  Pay attention to words like: 'must/must not', 'can/cannot', 'should/should not', 'need to', 'have to' which are moral indicators, pointing to what you believe is obligatory, forbidden, expected and permissible.
- What are the **contexts** of these judgements?
  Where does that (judgement or idea) come from? Whose voices do you hear (telling that rule)? What do they say? Where did you learn it? Who agrees?
- What were the **stories** connected to these judgements and rules?

Pearce and Cronen (1980) highlight that the contexts that inform our meanings and action do not hold equal impact. I (Catherine) was therefore curious about which contexts were contributing to Tamar's sense of 'difficulty' and what stories were connected to these contexts. Therefore, I invited Tamar to reflect on the contexts informing her judgements that 'this felt wrong . . . it is disgusting' and that 'Lisa should not be doing this to herself' with questions like: 'What are the contexts that speak to you about this feeling *wrong – disgusting*? For instance, what would your family, your culture, or maybe people from your community say?'

> Tamar said she had 'never thought about it like this before . . . it is very strange . . . but when I think about my culture and my family . . . they would be appalled, horrified if I did that to myself. Even tattooing is against our Jewish religion. I am not religious at all – but human branding has sickening connotations of the holocaust – they tattooed prisoners at Auschwitz [concentration camp] with a serial number, except if they were sent directly to the gas chambers.'

Catherine shows how she explores with curiosity the moral orders of Tamar's disgust through the different contexts of her life. Listening for the judgements Tamar is making and the rules informing her views of whether it is acceptable or even permissible to feel disgust in this situation enables Catherine to throw light on the many different and potentially contradictory rules about feeling 'disgusted and angry' with a client that Tamar holds from the multiple professional and personal contexts of her life.

Connecting with preferred professional identity

The judgements and rules we make about feeling or expressing emotions are generated and informed through the stories of our cultures and inform the stories we tell of our selves and our identities (Fredman, 2004). Thus, the stories we tell and the theories we have about arousal and disgust are intricately woven with our stories of identity and have implications for how we perceive the moral worth of ourselves. Since our intention is to enhance and not diminish or undermine supervisees' professional confidence and self-regard, we consider how supervisees' experiences, judgements and stories of arousal and disgust fit with their preferred view of self. We begin by learning what stories they want told about their self as a therapist, a professional and an ethical person, with questions like: 'How would you like to be viewed (by colleagues/clients/your profession)? How would you like (colleagues/clients/your profession) to talk about you?' If we are working with a new supervisee, we might ask: 'What would be useful for me to know about you and the way you work, such as your professional values, so I can keep them in mind while I listen to your dilemma?' We explore whether their experiences, judgements and stories enhance or diminish the abilities they want recognized with questions like: 'How does feeling/showing arousal/disgust in that situation fit with the story you would like told about yourself and the abilities you would like recognised?'

> Like Jacob and Glenda, Tamar questioned her own professional conduct, which left her feeling bad about herself as a therapist and unsure how to go on. She feared that her feelings of disgust could be viewed as 'allowing my prejudice about Lisa's lifestyle to affect the way I work with her – that is unethical – and really poor practice'.

It is through the medium of stories that we create ourselves, each other and the social worlds in which we live (Pearce, 1994). Thus, our stories shape our lives and are constitutive of our selves. They inform our actions and relationships with self and others (White and Epston, 1990). Tamar's Jewish cultural story gave meaning to her experiences of disgust and anger in relation to the human branding. However, informed by theories and guidelines of her profession, she negatively evaluated this *(social–moral) disgust* so that her judgement of her self evolved to inform a negative story of her professional identity, as a practitioner who was unprofessional, a poor fit with her preferred story of herself as an ethical practitioner, attentive to the therapeutic relationship and skilled at engaging clients. This negative self-story was not only distressing for Tamar, but was also interrupting her work with Lisa, blocking her curiosity about Lisa's story and her own responses to it, and leaving her uncertain of how to go on in the work.

We are committed to respecting supervisees' as well as clients' preferred cultural narratives. Therefore, when a supervisee's cultural or religious story conflicts with their professional ethical practice we do not challenge people's preferred stories, values or principles. Instead, we try to participate in the co-creation of stories which are different from the presenting self-diminishing narrative. That is, we participate in the construction of alternative stories that might open space for the creation of new meanings and hence new and preferred views of self as well as new possibilities for action. In supervision, therefore, our intention is to invite people to identify a range of stories, perhaps previously untold, from the different contexts of their life with a view to opening space for new meanings and alternative actions. By making sense of her response (disgust) to the human branding in the context of her cultural (holocaust) history, Tamar noted that she was able to 'be clearer what relates to my own issues and what relates to Lisa'. This exploration seemed to transform Tamar's experience of feeling 'appalled', 'disgusted' and 'angry' associated with human branding to 'something more like pain' so that Tamar became curious about why the pain did not feature in their conversation at all. She wanted to explore with Lisa whether she was aware of any pain – or only the heat and shaking she had described – and to check whether Lisa thought talking about pain (or not) could throw light on what they were addressing in the therapy at that moment.

Since Jacob described himself as 'unprofessional' and 'deskilled', I (Catherine) wanted to reconnect him to the professionalism that I genuinely thought he was demonstrating, but which he was concerned he had lost. I therefore asked him if he felt that overall the therapy was going well, which he thought it was, and we talked about the skills and approaches he had used as a therapist to help this. Once Jacob appeared to reconnect with his professional self, I invited him to speak from this position by asking him 'what preferred future he hoped for the client' and 'what kind of partner and relationship he hoped she would find' intending to encourage further his positioning as therapist (separate from potential partner), widen his perspective and encourage curiosity of his client's future life.

Inviting Jacob to give an account of his professional practice with his client, Leanne, and to take her perspective on her hopes for the future, reconnected him to his professional skills and the valuable and unique role he played in her life as her therapist. He remarked that he felt less aroused and, hence, less embarrassed when he now thought about Leanne. He went on to say that he anticipated finding it easier to manage feelings of arousal in the future by 'saying to myself this is my body responding normally – it doesn't mean I will act on this feeling' and 'if this doesn't work, I can always bring it to supervision'.

In conclusion

Many feelings can be elicited in therapy and brought to supervision, or evoked for the supervisee and supervisor within supervision itself. Perhaps two of the most difficult to openly discuss are feelings of arousal or disgust, and yet doing so is essential to maintaining curiosity and safety. Perhaps, because these feelings are not commonly felt in relation to clients, they catch us unawares, which can leave us feeling deskilled.

To have conversations about arousal and disgust in supervision requires trust and respect between the supervisee and supervisor. Therefore, as supervisors we try to honestly and openly explore the stories that connect with these feelings, linking these to our various contexts and considering how these fit or jar in our work. Once we have engaged in these explorations in supervision we often move on to consider whether our feelings, and the stories they connect with, could be resources to draw on in our work with our clients. In chapter 8, Jo Bownas offers a guide for supervisors to invite supervisees to approach their bodily experiences as a resource in 'body-focused supervision'.

References

Burnham, J. (2005) Relational reflexivity: a tool for socially constructing therapeutic relationships. In C. Flaskas, B. Mason and A. Perlesz (eds). *The Space Between.* London. Karnac.

Butler, C. (2010) Difference is within us. Keynote presentation. *British Association for Sexual and Relationship Therapy Conference*, Warwick, May 2010.

Butler, C. (2011). Breaking taboos: acknowledging therapist arousal and disgust. *Psychotherapy and Politics International*, 9(1), 61–6.

Cronen, V. E. and Lang, P. (1994) Language and action: Wittgenstein and Dewey in the practice of therapy and consultation. *Human Systems: The Journal of Systemic Consultation and Management*, 5, 5–43.

De Jong, P. J., van Lankveld, J., Elgersma, H. J. and Borg, C. (2010) Disgust and sexual problems: theoretical conceptualization and case illustration. *International Journal of Cognitive Therapy*, 3(1), 23–39.

Fredman, G. (1997) *Death Talk: Conversations with Children and Families*. London: Karnac.

Fredman, G. (2004) *Transforming Emotion: Conversations in Counselling and Psychotherapy.* London: Wiley & Sons.

Lang, P., Little, M. and Cronen, V. (1990) The systemic professionals: domains of action and the question of neutrality. *Human Systems: The Journal of Systemic Consultation and Management*, 1, 34–40.

Marzillier, J. (2010) *The Gossamer Thread: My Life as a Psychotherapist.* London: Karnac.

Oliver, C. (2005) *Reflexive Enquiry: A Framework for Consultancy Practice*. London: Karnac Books.

Pearce, W. B. and Cronen, V. (1980) *Communication, Action, and Meaning: The Creation of Social Realities.* New York: Praeger.

Pearce, W. B. (1994) *Interpersonal Communication: Making Social Worlds*. New York: HarperCollins.

Pope, K. S., Sonne, J. L. and Holroyd, J. (2005) *Sexual Feelings in Psychotherapy: Exploration for Therapists and Therapist-in-Training*. Washington, DC: American Psychological Association.

Pope, K. S. and Tabachnick, B. G. (1993) Therapists' anger, hate, fear and sexual feelings: national survey of therapist response, client characteristics, critical events, formal complaints, and training. *Professional Psychology, Research and Practice*, 24(2), 142–52.

Yalom, I. D. (2010) *The Gift of Therapy. An Open Letter to a New Generation of Therapists and Their Patients.* Revised and updated edition. London: Piatkus.

White, M. and Epston, D. (1990) *Narrative Means to Therapeutic Ends*. Adelaide: Dulwich Centre Publications.

10 Mindfulness

Bringing body and breath to supervision

Olga Levitt

This chapter explores how supervisors can use mindfulness-based practices and a mindfulness-informed approach to address stress and increase compassion in supervision. I describe my own journey with Mindfulness, with examples from supervision and therapy practice, in which attention to the breath is used to connect mind, body and emotion. I also address the challenges of introducing the body into talking therapy and supervision and suggest alternative practices when focusing on the breath may not be helpful.

My journey to Mindfulness in supervision

Working as a social worker and later as a systemic family therapist, in the challenging environment of child mental health public services in London, I turned to yoga to manage the pressures of my own work and life. Over the course of my training as a therapist, I experienced various forms of helpful therapy, but the yoga reached parts of me that talking therapies did not – my body! I came to appreciate that this was working directly with the body–mind connection.

My interest in this connection grew to such an extent that I decided to train as a yoga teacher. I soon noticed that the students who attended my yoga classes had problems as great and varied as those who consulted me as a therapist; and they seemed to be helped by the yoga. I became curious about what in the yoga practice made such a difference to people's ability to cope with life's stresses. I was also reading about the effective therapeutic work done by yoga teachers (Mason, 2015) and wanted to find ways of incorporating the inseparable body–mind in my therapy and supervision practice in a coherent way. Increasingly, I wanted to share my expertise from both my systemic psychotherapy and yoga teaching practices in appropriate ways – well aware that my therapy clients and supervisees did not come to me for yoga and my yoga students did not want to be 'theraped'. As so often happens, the initiative to incorporate yoga and Mindfulness into my therapy practice came from my clients and supervisees, who invited me into conversations and practices that I might not have felt permitted to introduce. One such invitation, that initially felt challenging to my professional boundaries with clients and the boundaries between yoga teaching and therapy, was an encounter with eight-year-old Jill.

> Jill's father brought her to see me shortly after the death of her mother. He was concerned that Jill was 'not talking about her own pain and loss' and 'trying to hold herself together for the sake of us [father and brothers]'. In our first session I noticed that Jill immediately deflected any talk she found difficult by changing the subject or physically moving. When I handed her father my business card after our session, Jill looked over his shoulder and asked, 'Do you teach yoga too? Can we do that?' I looked at her father, who nodded and so we agreed to include some yoga in our sessions. Soon I noticed that, despite being very flexible in her body, Jill was quick to move out of any position in which she was not immediately comfortable. I encouraged her to stay a little longer in physically challenging positions, showing her how to use her breath and notice how the feelings changed. Thus, Jill managed to stay in increasingly challenging postures, which soon translated into her ability to stay with more difficult conversations and feelings that she was able to go on to express in a subsequent family meeting.

This physical and emotional connection was exciting. I began to wonder how I could take this learning forward with other clients and supervisees. It was obviously not appropriate to suggest that all clients and supervisees bring yoga mats to sessions!

In Western society there has been a split between mind and body in our thinking and in our services, which may account for why it has been difficult to incorporate the body into talking therapies. In the context of this mind–body split it may not seem 'appropriate' for a 'talking therapist' to comment on, and certainly not to touch, another's body. Thus, introducing ideas about the body and putting them into practice can arouse anxiety in psychotherapists and is approached, appropriately, with caution. Mindfulness has given me an acceptable gateway into bringing the body more into my therapy practice, providing the bridge between body and mind, often via the breath, but also using all the senses: Mindfulness 'embodies bringing a gentle awareness to experience. It opens space for self and relational compassion. It fully embraces body, speech and mind as inseparable aspects of joint action' (Hannah, 2013).

What is Mindfulness?

Mindfulness means deliberately focusing one's attention on what is occurring in the present moment in a non-judgemental and accepting way. It incorporates both the careful *self-regulation of attention*, so that it is beamed onto immediate experience, and the *attitude of attention*, which is characterised by non-judgement, acceptance, loving-kindness and compassion (Kabat-Zinn, 1990).

I find it challenging to write about Mindfulness, as it is something that has to be experienced. So, before you continue to read this chapter, I invite you to pause and notice how you are sitting (or lying or standing) and take a moment to notice what you can sense in your body, what feelings are around for you and what thoughts are going through your head.

PAUSE

You may have welcomed the pause, or noticed an impatience, a wish to press on. Or you may have felt 'so what'. You may have noticed the ache in your neck. Or perhaps you chose to ignore the invitation to pause and continued reading. Whatever was happening for you, whatever you experienced or however you responded, just notice it and let it be. Mindfulness is observing your mind and your body in *this* moment without evaluating it or trying to change it.

Mindfulness meditation has its roots in Eastern philosophy and Buddhism. In the Western world it has been developed as a secular approach to health and social care and is used in education (mindfulnessinschools.org) and in business (Chaskalson, 2011). In the 1970s Jon Kabat-Zinn, a molecular biologist with experience in Buddhist meditation, developed a non-religious version of meditation which grew into the *Mindfulness-Based Stress Reduction* (MBSR) eight-week programme (Kabat-Zinn, 1990: 8). Many of the secular approaches, including my own, stem from this programme.

Mindfulness is both a process – *Mindful Practice* – and an outcome – *Mindful Awareness* (Shapiro and Carlson, 2009). We do formal and informal *mindful practices* in order to develop *mindful awareness*. Formal practices involve setting aside time each day to sit quietly in either a guided meditation or in silence. Formal practices can also involve *mindful movement* or *mindful walking*. Informal practices are the exercises we try to incorporate into our day in order to become aware of what we are sensing, feeling and thinking in any particular moment. Examples are pausing, as we have just done, or doing a particular activity (such as eating) with mindful awareness.

Mindfulness can give us the opportunity to notice how we go through much of life 'on automatic pilot'. By becoming alert to the detailed information from our bodies, through our senses, we can experience things differently and explore the possibility of *not reacting* purely out of habit. This gives us the chance to *respond* deliberately, rather than to *react* automatically. Thus, Mindfulness enables us to identify our own habitual patterns and opens space for us to explore alternate ways of being and doing, a valuable practice we might bring to supervision.

I began to convene *Mindfulness for Therapists* workshops to explore, use and develop mindfulness practices with supervisees and supervisor colleagues. Although I work in a systemic theoretical framework, my supervisees and workshop participants come from different theoretical backgrounds. We have found that the theory and practice of Mindfulness can bridge the gap, not only between body and mind, but also between different therapy orientations.

Bridging body and talk through Mindful Breathing in supervision

As far back as the early 1990s Tom Andersen (1991), a Norwegian psychiatrist and family therapist, was writing about bringing attention to our breath in psychotherapeutic practices. In his work with physiotherapists, Andersen learned how the body tenses and the breath is constricted with physical and psychic pain and discomfort. He noticed how 'inspiration,' in both senses of the word, is blocked when we are in difficulty. He learned how, in physical manipulation, pressure needs to be strong enough to stimulate pain to free up muscles but not too strong, as this would either cause further damage or have no effect. Drawing a parallel with the process of therapy, he showed how diligent observation of the physical and breathing response of clients can help therapists to know how to be in the dialogue. If a therapist's question or statement introduces a significant difference, the therapist may notice a sharp inhalation followed by an exhalation with the potential to heal. An intervention that is experienced as too different or too unusual (Andersen, 1991) will be reflected in a change of breathing and will stop the conversation. In my experience in supervision, careful following of the supervisee's breath can guide us in staying attuned to finding 'the difference that makes a difference' (Bateson, 1972).

> In a recent supervision session, two therapists described a family session in which they had been co-working. They were very perturbed by the behaviour of the identified client, a young man in his twenties, who had been pacing up and down the room during the session. They spoke about their desire to be 'sympathetic' and 'non-judgemental' and their awareness of 'the power' this young man was exerting in the room. I was about to explore their understanding of the meaning of the young man's behaviour, when I became aware of the physical restlessness of the two therapists. Therefore, responding to their bodies rather than what they were saying, I asked, 'Did you offer to walk with the young man?' Both supervisees inhaled sharply in response to my question. Then there was a pause as they exhaled, followed by a slowing of the tempo and softening of tone in the conversation.

My question, which also had an element of humour to it, seemed to relax and support the supervisees, bringing forth accounts of the many ways they had, metaphorically, 'walked alongside' the young man in the session; enabling them to describe appreciatively how they had worked creatively with an unusual challenge. Initially, I responded to unease in their bodies rather than to what the supervisees said or even how they expressed it. I tuned in to their considerable physical discomfort, addressing the physical challenge of how to bodily position oneself and conduct a session as a therapist with a 'rapidly pacing' client.

Paré *et al.* (2012) state that the aims of Mindfulness and the aims of therapy are 'attention, intention and an ethic of care'. In mindful supervision we aim to embody these attributes, as I hope I have illustrated in the example above, through my careful attention to the supervisees' embodiment and in caring for them and their client.

Therapists or supervisors who wish to use Mindfulness in their work with clients or supervisees need to have practiced Mindfulness for themselves. Mindfulness is not a technique that one can pluck out of the toolbox and use at will without having regular and ongoing experience of this approach or 'way of being in the world'. Drawing on Shapiro and Carlson's (2009) distinction between *mindfulness-based* and *mindfulness-informed* therapy, I distinguish between *mindfulness-based* and *mindfulness-informed* supervision. In *mindfulness-based* supervision the supervisor will explicitly teach or share mindful practices in the supervision session, as I did with Paul (below). In *mindfulness-informed* supervision, the supervisor will embody mindful ways of understanding and being in the supervision process without specifically teaching or sharing mindfulness practices with supervisees, as I describe in the example above.

Mindfulness-based supervision

It is important that supervisors and supervisees decide together whether the formal teaching and sharing of meditation practices are appropriate and useful in the supervision or therapy. As with all practices, this is not appropriate for all supervision or supervisees. In preparation for the conference that gave rise to this book (Friends of KCC, 2013), I asked my supervisees if, for a period, we could start each session with the *Three-Minute Breathing Space* (Segal *et al.*, 2002: 184), also known as the *Three-Step Breathing Space* (Exercise 10.1) (Centre for Mindfulness Research and Practice, undated: 33).

The breathing space is intended to provide the practitioner with a way of moving out of 'automatic pilot' mode and connecting with the present moment. Attention moves from wide (*Acknowledging*) to narrow (*Gathering*) and then to wide (*Expanding*), as sand moves through an hourglass.

You, the reader, may like to create a three-minute space while reading this chapter to practice this *Three-Step Breathing* exercise which can be found of page 136.

All the supervisees kindly agreed to try out this practice, which gave rise to useful feedback and a wide variety of responses. Some supervisees found it helpfully connected them with their 'gut reactions', 'religious beliefs' and 'spiritual resources'. Some felt it helped them slow down and listen to their bodies. One person said the practice was 'not for me – although other people may find it helpful'. Another, while not particularly enjoying the practice, was curious about what 'came up' for her, which she chose to reflect on herself, rather than share with me.

> Paul, a supervisee, described himself as 'very stressed' and was not sure if he could 'focus or think' in supervision. He asked if we could start our session with a brief 'guided relaxation'. When I explored 'what sort of relaxation' Paul was referring to, he clarified 'progressive muscle relaxation' (Ost, 1987) which he hoped might help him 'de-stress'. I invited Paul to join me in 'a simple exercise, which can help to ground us so we are more able to be present and to focus, by bringing

our attention to our body and bringing awareness to the breath' (Exercise 10.2). I also explained that this exercise was different from relaxation since 'we are not particularly trying to relax but rather to be aware, to be mindful of whatever arises. Letting go allows us to be open to whatever is there'. Paul was keen to participate.

When I introduce formal mindfulness exercises, like Exercises 10.1 and 10.2, with supervisees and clients I always explain that I will do the practice myself alongside them and that I do not look at them. I emphasise that there is no right way to do the practice.

Exercise 10.1 Three-Step Breathing Space

Sit on a chair with your feet on the ground. Eyes can be closed or cast downwards.

1 Acknowledging

Bring yourself into the present moment by connecting with the ground and any solid surface with which your body is in contact.

Deliberately adopt a lengthened and dignified posture. Then ask:

'What is going on for me right now?'

Acknowledge any sensations in the body, any thoughts and emotions.

Stay with them for a few moments. Notice everything including negative feelings or experiences. Allow it all to be present.

2 Gathering

Turn your attention to your breath.

Gently focus on each in-breath and each out-breath.

Follow your breath as it comes in and goes out, one breath after another.

The breath can be an *anchor* to bring you into the present moment, to help you connect to a state of awareness and stillness.

3 Expanding

Expand your awareness of your breath to awareness of the whole body as if the whole body were breathing. Become aware of your body in space and become aware of your facial expression.

Expand your awareness to the space in front of you, behind you, on either side of you and below and above you.

Exercise 10.2 Awareness of body and breath

Sit on a chair with legs uncrossed and feet firmly placed on the floor.

Feel your seat on the chair and if possible have your back self-supporting away from the back of the chair.

Assume an upright, dignified, yet relaxed position.

Eyes can be closed or cast downwards.

Feel your feet on the ground.

Be aware of the contact of your body with the chair, allowing the body to settle.

Against that grounded feeling, letting the spine lengthen from the tailbone right up to the top of the head. With a firm base and back, allowing the front body to soften and open.

Bringing your attention to your breath. If it helps you to feel the breath, have your hands flat against your belly, middle fingers meeting at the navel.

Feeling the breath coming in and going out.

Feeling the breath rather than thinking about the breath.

Sit like this for a few minutes.

Let your awareness of your breath fade into the background.

Become aware of your body on the chair, your feet on the floor, of yourself sitting in this room.

Become aware of the sounds you can hear, both near and far.

Drop your chin to your chest and slowly open your eyes if they have been closed and when you are ready raise your head.

This mindfulness practice was acceptable to Paul, perhaps because it did not appear too different from his familiar relaxation practice and the intention of the exercise was coherent with the outcome he wanted. Paul noticed that his breath and heart rate slowed. He described feeling calmer. I observed that he was able to take a different position when talking about the stresses of his work – more of a distance from the stresses rather than being in the stress and overwhelmed by it.

When breathing practices do not fit, for example for people who experience breathing difficulties or severe tinnitus (like Fran p. 140), we can offer alternative exercises that invite mindful attention to external stimuli, like listening to the sounds around, or to different bodily sensations like the sensation of holding an object such as a stone in the hand.

Shrinking stress and growing attention and compassion with supervisees

Often practitioners, like Paul, come to supervision distressed by the experience of being with clients' suffering, as well as stressed by pressures in the workplace, such as re-structuring, cut-backs, demands to see more clients and provide detailed documentation for monitoring of their clinical activity. 'Burnout' and 'compassion fatigue' often show up as embodied symptoms, such as backache and frequent illness. As a supervisor, I have used mindfulness practices as one way of addressing this sort of stress with supervisees.

Burnham (2005) describes how therapists can 'warm the context' to improve the *readiness* of clients toward therapeutic work through enquiry about the usefulness and experience of the praxis for the clients. He also emphasises the importance of moving at the pace and tempo set by the client within the particular episode. I have found that a brief shared mindfulness practice can have the effect of physically and mentally attuning supervisor and supervisee and 'warming the context' for the ongoing conversation and readiness to meet clients in a different way: one that involves changing the body–mind state of the participants, thereby enabling them to be more open to the conversation that follows. Starting the session like this 'warmed the context' and enabled a more relaxed and reflective conversation to take place with Paul.

Supervision can make an important contribution to developing and maintaining the consistent attention and compassion expected of therapists (Morgan *et al.*, 2013). With the development of meditation practices specifically geared to increasing compassion (Lutz *et al.*, 2009, cited in Lazar, 2013), mindfulness practice can make a valuable contribution to compassion-focused supervision. Following the supervision session in which we practised *Awareness of Body and Breath*, Paul remarked, at his next supervision, that he had found himself 'more open to what [his clients] were feeling'. He explained, 'Relaxation exercises always help me relax. That breathing [Exercise 10.2] was different – it helped me be there, open, for my clients.'

For thousands of years, practitioners have claimed that meditation can bring about a wide range of changes in body and mind, but it is only in recent years that these claims have been evaluated scientifically. Research supports that mindfulness practice decreases stress levels in the body with even relatively brief practice (Hölzel *et al.*, 2010, cited in Lazar, 2013). For example, MBSR subjects' brains and their relationship to the environment changed after practicing Mindfulness for only eight weeks, even when their external stressful environment had not changed (Lazar, 2013). Areas of the brain (the anterior insula and sensory cortex) involved in observing internal and external physical sensations have been shown to have increased cortical thickness in long-term meditators (Lazar *et al.*, 2005) suggesting meditation practice could encourage supervisees to develop their powers of observation, of both their own bodies and those of their clients. One of the challenges for researchers, and a difficulty in interpreting the research, is that there are many different forms of meditation. However, what is of particular interest to us as therapists and supervisors is that, with regular meditation, people report they are better able to cope with difficult situations, can concentrate better, have improved memory and have more empathy and compassion.

> Ilana, who was completing her Masters training in counselling, wanted to use supervision to prepare for a piece of course work. She looked close to tears and told me that she 'gets very anxious' whenever she has to submit an assignment. I invited her to join me in a mindfulness practice, 'Awareness of Body and Breath', to connect her with the way the 'anxious' feelings were manifesting in her body, mind and emotions (Exercise 10.2).

I intended to offer Ilana this simple exercise to help her ground her body by focusing awareness on her feet on the floor and her body contact with the chair, and by bringing her awareness to the breath. Initially Ilana's heightened awareness of her heart beating loudly and rapidly startled her, so that she questioned whether the exercise was helping. Therefore, through a process of *Mindful Enquiry*, I invited her to attend to her physical experience (*'Can you describe how your heart sounded?' 'Where were you feeling it?'*); make sense of her 'loud and fast beating heart' (*'Was it a familiar or unusual feeling?' 'What were you expecting to happen?'*), and make links between what she had noticed and discovered (*'What do you think would have to happen for you to feel it was helpful?'*), until she and I were able to contemplate, 'Isn't it interesting that you are breathing and your heart is beating all the time and you are unaware of it, but when you stop and focus your attention it sounds so loud. What does that lead you to think in terms of where we place attention?'

With repeated practice in our supervision sessions, Ilana noticed her attention shifting and her breath calming. She reported that she still 'felt anxious', but that by connecting with the bodily sensations, rather than trying to 'push them away', she was able to separate out the physical experiences, the emotions and the thoughts, enabling her to change her relationship with the feelings so that she did not find them so debilitating. By grounding herself in her body and using her breath as a stable point to which she could return, she felt more in control of the 'anxious feelings'.

Focusing awareness on body and breath can help to bring attention away from thoughts and into the body, to re-position supervisees in relation to their own processes. Whatever happens for supervisees and supervisors during this practice, it tends to slow things down and bring a calmness and deliberateness, yet gentleness, to the conversation that follows. Whatever happens is information.

> After using this practice regularly and finding it so helpful, Ilana wanted to share the practice with a client. However, she expressed concern that her client 'might not like the practice or even refuse to do it'. This

approach of teaching a physical practice felt very different for Ilana and therefore 'risky'. Therefore, we spent time in supervision talking about introducing the idea and also discussed the importance of *Mindful Enquiry* after mindfulness practice.

Mindful Enquiry

The process of enquiry is important when working with mindfulness practices in therapy or supervision. The enquiry encompasses three inter-connecting reflexive layers:

- *Encouraging the noticing* of direct experiences, including bodily sensations, thoughts and feelings.
- *Dialoguing* – by placing the direct noticing in a personal and professional context of understanding.
- *Linking* what has been noticed to the current task in supervision and to recurrent patterns in the supervisee's professional practice.

(Centre for Mindfulness Research and Practice, 2012. See Guide 10.1 for examples of *Mindful Enquiry* questions.)

I shared the 'ticking clock' story from my own therapeutic practice with Ilana to illustrate *Mindful Enquiry* and to show that there is no specific desired outcome, but that we are using *Mindful Enquiry* to explore and possibly develop the mind–body connection, whatever happens in the practice.

The ticking clock

Fran, a woman in her fifties, came to see me as she was 'struggling in a new relationship' and 'panicking about deadlines' at work. Fran's usual pattern was to begin speaking rapidly as soon as she arrived for her session, sometimes even before she had taken off her coat. One day I suggested we slow down and try the Awareness of Body and Breath (Exercise 10.2). We were no more than a few seconds into the practice when she sat bolt upright, opened her eyes and informed me she could not do it. She explained that she suffered from tinnitus (ringing in the ears) and that sitting quietly, as we had done, was unbearable for her. I had not known about the tinnitus. Fran had previously told me she collected clocks and that 'the ticking clocks all over [her] house' was 'an area of contention' with her new boyfriend who found the ticking very irritating. I wondered aloud whether Fran had planned to have the constant sound of ticking to mask the ringing in her ears. Fran had not previously made this connection, but agreed that the ticking did help her. When she later told her boyfriend that the ticking sounds helped to mask the tinnitus, it changed the meaning of the sounds for him too.

Guide 10.1 *Mindful Enquiry*: guiding questions

Encouraging the noticing

- *What did you notice in your body – physical sensations including sounds, colours, textures, movement?*
- *Where in the body did you notice that?*
- *What did those sensations in the body tell you about your emotions in the moment?*
- *Did the sensations change during the practice?*
- *What thoughts were going through your head – memories, worries, planning, daydreams, food, shopping lists?*

Dialoguing

- *Were you surprised by your response?*
- *Was the feeling familiar to you?*
- *Have there been other times you were aware of those experiences? (If so) what was happening for you then?*
- *Did you notice any words, phrases or images that came up which particularly resonated for you?*

Linking

- *How do the sensations/emotions/thoughts you have noticed, relate to the issues you have brought to supervision today?*
- *Was there anything you noticed that particularly interested you?*
- *As you reflect on your experience today, are there any connections that you can make to other conversations we have had, or you have had with clients?*

This story shows how the enquiry following mindfulness practice can enable us to explore the person's experience of the practice and also make connections with the issues the client or supervisee brings for help. The enquiry after mindfulness practice intends to draw out whatever the person has noticed during the practice and to encourage reflection on their experience. By guiding the supervisee's exploration of their experience and embodying compassionate, non-judgemental curiosity, supervisors can explore through dialogue together with supervisees, linking observations and discoveries to the aims of supervision. By closely tracking the supervisee's responses, the supervisor can use Mindfulness and supervisory skills to sense whether an enquiry is appropriate or not, both before and in the process of the enquiry. *Mindful Enquiry* should not become an interrogation. The supervisor takes a curious, not-knowing position, not needing to guide the conversation to any particular outcome. The enquiry aims to open space for creating and recognising possibilities. If supervisees do not want to talk about their experience at all, this wish is respected as each person's experience is honoured.

Supervisees have generally valued my sharing formal mindfulness practices. However, pressure of time poses a common challenge in supervision. Supervisees often come to supervision with many issues they want to address, including complex caseloads and complicated agency relationships, so that beginning supervision with a mindfulness exercise can feel like 'a waste of precious supervision time' or 'a luxury', albeit a useful one. I have learned that sharing my passion for Mindfulness in an evangelical way is not helpful to supervisees. Rather it needs to grow organically from the work; timing and 'warming the context' for the mindfulness practice are important.

It is not necessary to incorporate formal practices in order to bring Mindfulness and body awareness into supervision. Informed by our own mindfulness practice, supervisors can embody mindful awareness by accepting what is. In mindfulness-informed supervision, supervisors hold a belief in the essential good nature and inter-connectedness of all beings. Conscious of both the impermanent and paradoxical nature of experience, supervisors intend to consciously respond from a position of curiosity rather than automatically react (Shapiro and Carlson, 2009).

Mindfulness-informed supervision

In my efforts to be a Mindfulness-informed supervisor, I try to keep an open compassionate awareness to what is happening in my mind and body and in relation to supervisees. For example, before a supervision session I spend some time grounding myself by connecting with mindful awareness to my feet on the floor and my body in contact with the chair and bringing my attention to my breath (as in Exercise 10.1). I remind myself to try to keep this embodied presence. Inevitably, where we choose to place our awareness is formed by who we are, including our race, gender, culture, age, religion, sexuality and so on. How we embody our world and how we interpret the way others embody, is socially constructed. Mindfulness teaches us that 'thoughts are only thoughts; they are not facts – even the ones that say they are' (Segal *et al.*, 2002: 244). This reminds us to remain irreverent, tentative and **curious** about our own processes and observations.

I want to tell you about my own experience when I began to practice mindfulness meditation and how it informed my supervision practice. Although I had practiced yoga for many years, when I began a formal mindfulness meditation practice I quickly noticed that I was very irritable and quite agitated, much more so than normal and to an extent that my family noticed it too. When I began to reflect on this by **noticing what was happening in my body** and how this was connecting with my thoughts and feeling, I realised that deep yoga breathing had been very efficient in calming me down and that my pattern in relationships is to try to smooth things over and 'make things better'. When I began to notice my natural breath and **accept things as they were**, I realised there were things going on in my life with which I was not happy and which needed to be addressed rather than smoothed over. I now had the possibility of **consciously responding** differently rather than falling into my automatic default mode.

Curious about whether I repeated this pattern of behaviour in my work as a supervisor, I focused my awareness on the times in a supervision conversation where I stayed with a supervisee's difficulty, exploring it, and times I 'tried to make things better'. I used the awareness of my body and breath and that of my supervisees to slow things down and make conscious choices moment by moment. Each meditator will make his or her own discoveries!

The mindfulness concepts of 'accepting things just as they are – not striving to make things different' (Kabat-Zinn, 1990: 37), have become a mantra for me. When I notice my shoulders tensing and butterflies in my stomach, I check in with what is going on and, particularly, whether I and/or my supervisee are trying to help too much. **Accepting** suggests a way of openly relating to experience whatever is there, rather than closing down or fighting it. When we stop struggling and stay with what is already there, we have the opportunity to view and relate to our issues with greater clarity and freedom. This comes from the belief that we are who we need to be in any given moment and that all our healing and learning is already present.

This enables us to be curious and explore from a **compassionate** position – compassion for the supervisee and the clients. We are also appreciative of the supervisee, not in a superficial way but by carefully enquiring about their experience.

> Angela, a very mild-mannered supervisee, came into a supervision session telling me she was 'still seething' from a home-visit she had made the previous day. It was the first time I had heard Angela express angry feelings about a client and I was very curious about what had happened. Angela was upset with herself for 'getting so angry and worked up'. I asked her to **stay with** the 'angry and worked up' feeling so we could explore it. Angela spoke about her 'rage' with a mother of a young boy who was having difficulty getting into school. They had had what felt like a very productive positive session and then right at the end of the meeting the mother had said, 'of course it won't work' and had continued to 'overturn everything' they had discussed. Angela spoke about feeling the tension rise in her body so that she wanted to leave quickly 'before I said or did something I would regret'.
>
> I asked her what she had felt like doing and she said 'shaking the mother'.

Informed by the **belief that we can hold paradoxical feelings**, I invited **curiosity** about 'whether fear was alongside anger in the shaking'. **Acknowledging the interdependence of all beings**, I wondered, 'Who else might feel like shaking whom?' which opened space for us to explore the physicality of each person involved and, if there was fear, 'Who was fearful and about what or of whom?' Having noticed Angela's own unhappiness at her strong reaction, **embodying compassionate awareness**, I wondered if the boy and his mother might both also be upset with *themselves* for having strong reactions. Angela commented that the physical sensations in her body had changed over the course of our conversation.

> The next time I saw Angela she told me she had seen the family again. This time she was 'much more aware of how worried' the mother was about her son. She had chosen to teach mother and son a relaxation exercise together to help the boy to address the 'panic' going into school and for the mother to join in so she could help him practice. The mother was pleased that Angela had taken her worries about her son seriously and given them both something they could do about it.

This example also raises the interesting question, familiar to therapists and supervisors, of whether to move away from painful, sometimes traumatic experiences or whether to stay with them and explore them with the hope they are transformed in the process. When a person is meditating alone she has the choice about how much she wants to 'come up close to the difficulty', whether to stay there or move away as attention shifts and returns and dances around an issue. In supervision we negotiate that dance together, paying careful attention to body and breath.

In order to develop reflective practitioners, Schon (1983) suggests promoting increased reflexivity on the part of professionals by inviting them to be more mindful. As a mindfulness-informed supervisor, I slow the process down and create pauses and space for reflection. Noticing the way sensations in the body change from moment to moment and how our thoughts continually pass through our minds, fits with my systemic social constructionist approach, in which we view our 'selves' as being continually constructed and re-constructed in conversation. In becoming mindful of our own body–mind processes we can become aware of how we continually construct and re-construct our view of 'self' and, for supervisees, our view of 'self as therapist' in our internal conversation. The body can give us strong messages, often before the mind is even aware of something. Alternatively, the mind can interpret the messages in a certain way (as with Angela, the self-criticism: '*I am not a good therapist for getting worked up*'). If we stay compassionately with the experience and how it changes in the body, moment to moment, like Angela was able to do with the support of supervision, we may become aware that there are other equally valid thoughts.

Final reflections

The emphasis in Mindfulness is to focus on the detailed information we are receiving in the moment, initially through our bodies. Although therapists have often broken down interactions into the detail of what is happening, moment by moment, we have tended to neglect the information we all receive through our senses, our breath and our bodies. The body can give us strong messages, often before the mind is even aware of something. Noticing both our own and the supervisee's embodiment and breath patterns will bring awareness to potentially transformative points where conversations can take new directions. By deliberately developing mindful awareness, we have a way of enhancing our supervision and therapeutic practice, as well as our relationships with our colleagues, leading to calmer, less adversarial and kinder conversations.

Before we end, I invite you once more to:

PAUSE

Notice any sensations in your body. Notice your feelings, and the thoughts passing through your mind – making space for it all.

References

Andersen, T. (1991) *The Reflecting Team: Dialogues and Dialogues About the Dialogues.* London: Norton.

Bateson, G. (1972) *Steps to an Ecology of Mind.* New York. Ballantine.

Burnham, J. (2005) Relational reflexivity: a tool for socially constructing therapeutic relationships. In C. Flaskas, B. Mason and A. Perlesz (eds). *The Space Between.* London: Karnac.

Centre for Mindfulness Research and Practice, School of Psychology, Bangor University (undated) *Mindfulness-Based Stress Reduction Course Information.* Bangor, Wales.

Centre for Mindfulness Research and Practice, School of Psychology, Bangor University. (2012) *Teacher Training Retreat for Mindfulness-based Teacher: Resource Pack.* Bangor, Wales.

Chaskalson, M. (2011) *The Mindful Workplace: Developing Resilient Individuals and Resonant Organizations with MBSR.* Oxford:Wiley-Blackwell.

Friends of KCC (2013) *Embodiment in Supervision Conference.* London.

Hannah, C. (2013) The Practice of Mindfulness as a Context for Grounded Reflexivity. Workshop. *Embodiment in Supervision Conference.* London: Conway Hall.

Hölzel, B., Carmody, J., Evans, K. Hoge, E., Dusek, J., Morgan, L., Pitman, R. K. and Lazar, S. W. (2010) Stress reduction correlates with structural changes in the amygdala. *Social Cognitive and Affective Neuroscience*, 5, 11–17.

Kabat-Zinn, J. (1990) *Full Catastrophe Living.* London: Piatkus.

Lazar, S. W. (2013) The neurobiology of Mindfulness. In C. K. Germer, R. D. Siegel and P. R Fulton (eds). *Mindfulness and Psychotherapy.* New York: Guilford Press.

Lazar, S. W., Kerr, C. E., Wasserman, R. H., Gray, J. R., Greve, D. N., Treadway, M. T., McGarveye, M., Quinnd, B. T., Dusekf, J. A., Bensonf, H., Raucha, S. L., Mooreh, C. I. and Fischl, B. (2005) Meditation experience is associated with increased cortical thickness. *NeuroReport*, 16(17), 1893–97.

Lutz, A., Greischar, L., Rawlings, N., Perlman, D. and Davidson, R. (2009) BOLD signal in insula is differentially related to cardiac functioning during compassion meditation in experts vs novices. *NeuroImage*, 47(3), 1038–46.

Mason, H. (2015) www.yogaforthemind.info; www.health.harvard.edu/mindand-mood/ yoga-for-anxiety-and-depression. Accessed June 2015.

Morgan, W. D., Morgan, S. T. and Germer, C. K. (2013) Cultivating attention and compassion in Mindfulness and psychotherapy. In C. K. Germer, R. D. Siegel and P. R. Fulton (eds). *Mindfulness and Psychotherapy.* New York: Guilford Press.

Ost, J. G. (1987) Applied relaxation: description of a coping technique and review of controlled studies, *Behavioural Research and Therapy*, 25, 397–410.

Paré, D. A., Richardson, B. and Tarragona, M. (2012) *Watching the Train: Mindfulness and Inner Dialogue in Therapist Skill Training.* (Online) (Accessed 9 March 2015) Available from www.glebeinstitute.com/writings/pare.htm

Schon, D. A. (1983) *The Reflective Practitioner: How Professionals Think in Action.* London: Basic Books.

Segal, Z. V., Williams, J. M. G. and Teasdale, J. D. (2002) *Mindfulness-Based Cognitive Therapy for Depression: A New Approach to Preventing Relapse.* London: The Guilford Press.

Shapiro, S. L. and Carlson, L. E. (2009) *The Art and Science of Mindfulness: Integrating Mindfulness into Psychology and the Helping Professions.* American Psychological Association.

Shapiro, S. L., Carlson, L. E., Astin, J. A. and Freedman, B. (2006) Mechanisms of Mindfulness. *Journal of Clinical Psychology*, 62(3), 373–86.

11 Continuing the conversation

Reflecting on embodiment in supervision

Jo Bownas and Glenda Fredman

> My (Jo's) starting point with this chapter was with my own body, the body not of a therapist or supervisor but of an author and editor of this book. Weighed down by work and various domestic emergencies, the all too imminent deadline for writing this chapter felt terrifying, and my body responded by freezing, closing down all thought and imagination, and separating me from the many resonances and excited responses I had previously felt reading these chapters. As I re-read the chapters my attention was scattered, and focused more on my watch than on the beautiful ideas that were before me.

Our bodies, presence and participation

The authors who contributed to Part II of this book approach the body as an important context through which we experience the world and connect in relationship. They offer examples of how, as practitioners and supervisors, our bodily experiences can interfere with our ability to be present and make a connection with the people with whom we work, in a similar way to how Jo's 'freezing' body 'closed down all thought and imagination . . . separating [her] from the many resonances and excited responses' she had previously felt for the chapters of this book.

We were struck by how many authors in this book share experiences of noxious physical symptoms during or after therapy or supervision sessions in response to witnessing or participating in stories of pain and suffering. For example, feeling 'sick in my stomach before each session' (Taiwo); 'intense feeling of nausea and faintness', 'feverish, nauseous and aching' (Jo) and 'wanting to retch' (Glenda). Often, when injured or feeling ill we would 'discount' or 'try desperately to counter' our bodily experience 'battling . . . to be alright for sessions'.

> In my work in a forensic setting there are times when I (Jo) experience, or witness in my supervisees, a physiological response to hearing the details of a particularly shocking act of violence committed by one of our clients (on another person or on him- or herself): our faces may contort,

our bodies fold in and pull back; we may feel nauseous. We may describe feeling 'revolted', 'sickened', 'disgusted' which, I think, is what Catherine and Glenda name as 'core disgust'. Like Glenda in her 'Toe in a bucket of blood' story we worry that our bodily responses may 'show' and may get in the way of our 'being with' our clients in therapy as we would wish to be. Sometimes our feelings are so strong that we recognise in ourselves a real reluctance to do the work, or to meet with the person whose actions have given rise to such feelings.

'Moving away' or coming up close

Olga Levitt (chapter 10) identifies a dilemma familiar to therapists and supervisors of whether to 'move away' from painful traumatic experiences or whether to 'come up close', staying with them and exploring the experiences in the hope they are transformed in the process.

In supervision, my (Jo's) approach is one of *accepting* strong feelings like 'disgust', thinking with supervisees how they can go on in the work despite the feelings. This might involve deciding whether there is someone in the team whose feelings are less overpowering and who might, therefore, take the lead in the work; or it might involve deciding to start the work knowing that our feelings of disgust will be present but knowing, too, that these feelings will come to dominate less once we have entered conversation with the person. In supervision I invite my supervisees to speak of what they know of the person apart from the ('disgusting') act, intending to separate the person from their actions and enable the supervisee to 'thicken' their description of the client.

Reflecting now, in the light of Catherine and Glenda's chapter, it occurs to me that I usually show little curiosity about the feelings of disgust, perhaps because I often share the feeling and so assume I 'know' what my supervisee is experiencing and what this means to her. I wonder what might emerge if, instead of 'taking for granted' those feelings, we came up a little closer and explored them together, asking in detail about the supervisee's bodily experience and expression, what stories these may connect with and what stories they invite about the supervisee and about her client. We might also wonder about what feelings the client may experience in listening to an account of his actions: would they be the same or different from ours?

In the secure hospital where I (Jo) work, our colleagues, our institution and the society that commissions our work expect us to manage our own feelings of 'core disgust' and not bring these to our work; but they also *expect* us to hold a position of 'social moral disgust'. If we stray too far from this position by, for instance, telling stories of our clients' abilities and moral commitments, or expressing feelings of warmth towards our clients, we may be accused of 'colluding', of becoming 'over-involved'; of 'ignoring', 'forgetting' or 'over-looking' the 'seriousness of the offence'. Supervisees working in child protection services, monitoring perpetrators of abuse, describe similar experiences to me. In these situations the experience or expression of disgust may distance us from our clients, but *not* expressing disgust may distance us from our colleagues and from societal approval. Catherine and Glenda's contextualising practices (chapter 9) offer me a way forward to explore the choices we have about how to position ourselves in relation to our judgements about strong feelings like disgust. They invite their supervisees to explore the personal and professional contexts of the judgements that inform or shape their feelings of disgust. Following their lead I could explore 'disgust' with a supervisee through her personal and professional contexts including her relationships with colleagues and the service.

Treating our bodies like machines in the workplace

Taiwo Afuape (chapter 7) warns us of the potential 'dangerous' consequences of treating our bodies as machines that have no life in them. She drew our attention to how often, in our work contexts, we are 'encouraged to think of bodily senses as unimportant background' to our lives. I (Glenda) reflected on my own tendency over the years towards devaluing my body in the work place, reducing it to a 'vehicle, commodity or consumer' (Afuape); recalling hundreds of meetings in which colleagues and I scoffed down sandwiches at great pace, whilst at the same time witnessing and swallowing stories of severe illness, disability, violence or abuse of the children we work with, like the following example:

> It was our lunchtime referrals meeting and, as usual, we were eating our lunch while reading referral letters, discussing how to respond, what we could offer and to whom to allocate the work. All team members had full caseloads with several people waiting for an appointment. The team leader had read out a request for an urgent appointment for an eight-year-old boy who had recently been diagnosed with a debilitating form of arthritis. His mother was described as 'devastated' and 'unable to stop herself crying'. The boy was 'refusing to attend school' and 'clinging desperately to his mother'. We also learned that the previous year the mother had witnessed the boy's father 'stabbed to death' in a knife attack. There was general agreement that the family could benefit from a quick response; however none of the team members had 'capacity' to offer the appointment. The conversation drifted to suggestions to 'refer on' to a neighbouring hospital, to recommend the mother 'get help for herself' from her GP counsellor, and to ask our physiotherapy and occupational therapy colleagues to 'assess' the boy. As this conversation developed I found myself feeling nauseous to the point I had to run out of the room. In the staff washroom I was overwhelmed by tears.

Since we experience our worlds through our bodies, and the body is central to the story telling process, not taking care of our bodies, not listening to our bodies can interfere with our ability to be present to the people we work with. In chapter 8,

Jo gives the example of how back pain rendered her 'stiff and lifeless' finding it 'hard to make a connection with the people with whom I am talking'. Taiwo notes that we are more likely to connect more fully with others when we feel less alienated from ourselves, and Jo points to the value of listening to our bodies since our experience of strong symptoms might be our 'body readying itself, through sickness, to retreat from what we are intending to do'. The nausea overwhelming my body in the team meeting literally contributed to my 'retreat' from the situation.

We make connections with Kaethe Weingarten's warning that clinicians can develop apathy as a numbing strategy when confronted with hopelessness and a seemingly impossible task. The apathy, numbness and indifference can pull us away from our 'crucial task' as a practitioner, which is to accompany the people with whom we work through suffering and hopelessness and to 'always be aware and empowered witnesses' (Weingarten, 2010: 11). The chapters in Part II remind us of the importance of our responsibility for 'accompaniment', as supervisors, to 'be truly present' to the supervisee to make it possible for the supervisee to accompany the client.

Staying present to witness and accompany

The authors of this section offer many examples of supervisees bringing to supervision their difficulty with staying present to witness and accompany clients. I (Glenda) am grateful to the authors of these chapters since the episode that follows occurred after reading their chapters, which helped me, as the clinical supervisor of the team, to 'stay present' and accompany my colleagues so they could move on from numbness and avoidance to accompany the child and his mother to find a way forward through their very distressing situation.

> I remained a little longer in the staff washroom. With the help of Taiwo and Olga's chapters, I stayed with the 'felt sense' focusing on what it felt like in my body and trying to 'listen' to what came from it. An image came forth of a tennis match; a child's face appeared on the ball. I remained looking at the ball and then turned my attention to my breath. I spent a few more minutes engaging with 'Awareness of body and breath' (Exercise 10.2). When I returned to my team, the discussion was focusing on 'where to refer' the boy. Mindful of the importance of entering the conversation with 'kindly awareness', I asked in a quiet, 'kind' voice, 'Are **we** playing tennis with this little boy?' The team leader looked distraught. Breathing in sharply, as if catching her breath in shock, she replied, 'What can I do – we have no one who can see this family'. A junior team member breathed out sighing, 'I don't think I can manage this on my own.' The conversation moved on to how we could address this dilemma with the referrer; whether we might contact the mother to explain there is a long wait, explore who is available to be with her at this difficult time, and whether we might offer the family an option of an

appointment at very short notice if someone cancels late. The team agreed that two practitioners would meet jointly with the family for the initial appointment.

These chapters brought into focus for us the importance of accompaniment to the therapeutic process and hence the importance of the supervisor's accompaniment, 'being truly present' to the supervisee to make it possible to accompany the client. Kaethe Weingarten (2010: 19–21) gives us pointers for how to support supervisees and ourselves, as supervisors and practitioners, to stay present, accompany and 'maintain a practice of reasonable hope' including: 'believing the small is not trivial'; holding modest expectations of success; seeing and hearing signs of reasonable hope; welcoming joy; enjoying vicarious hope; and recognising and resisting what is unjust or unfair. The authors contributing to Part II share a repertoire of practices to further enhance our ability to offer accompaniment and to bear witness (Weingarten, 2003). Their examples, exercises and guides enable us to engage with and listen to our body during sessions with clients and supervisees, invite supervisees to tune in to their bodies so they can connect with others and counter the critical gaze on our bodies by creating an atmosphere of kindly awareness, non-judgemental attitude and acceptance. Below, Jo gives an example of how she made use of these exercises to resolve the 'freezing' she described at the start of this chapter and to reconnect her with the chapters in Part II.

As Olga and Taiwo's words began to reach me (Jo), inviting me to focus attention 'on what is occurring in the present moment in a non-judgemental and accepting way' and to allow 'something useful to float up from a bodily sense, by bypassing the confused clutter of the mind', I decided to experiment with using the Focusing exercise (7.1) Taiwo offers. Exploring my 'felt sense', I allowed a merging of bodily sensation and emotion and let words and images arise: the words 'clenched' and 'scrunched up' came to me, followed by an image of a screwed-up sheet of paper, which seemed to resonate with my felt sense. Following Taiwo's exercise, I 'asked the felt sense' what it needed and the answer seemed to be that it needed to be smoothed out, opened up. At that moment I became distracted by noises from the street and got up to close the window. I noticed the screws in the window handle were loose and, though I have noticed and ignored this many times before, I immediately fetched a screwdriver and tightened the screws. As I became aware of how this activity connected with the felt sense I had just been exploring I began to smile and then to laugh, spontaneously stretching my 'clenched' jaw. It seemed that while I tightened the screws I was simultaneously loosening my body. Intrigued and encouraged by the 'mystery' (Afuape) of this process I decided to engage in the mindful breathing exercise offered by Olga (Exercise 10.1) to see if this might further help with the 'smoothing out' of my felt sense. As I focused my attention on my breathing, intentionally breathing into the 'scrunched' parts of my body, I felt myself expanding, unfolding. When I returned to the task of writing I found myself open afresh to the wonderful ideas contained in these chapters and to my own resonances and where they had taken me.

Guided by Jo's body-focused supervision (Guide 8.1), I (Glenda) noticed my own embodied responses as I read her account above. The images and connections to her body drew me in and I found myself 'unscrunching' and 'rescrunching' as I read. I noticed that reading this chapter from these different embodied positions or states ('scrunched' and 'un-scrunched') influenced my relationship with the words on the page and the ideas and connections they evoked for me. I decided to share my responses with Jo (via an email) and as I wrote I started to make connections with my own work and writing experiences. I became aware that in different bodily positions I was embodying different audiences to our book. At one point, embodying the critical voice of a former teacher, words on the page jarred and I found myself focusing on what I did not like. As my body embraced the warming generous smile of an encouraging senior colleague, whose discourse fits more closely with our approach, I felt a strong sense of joy, excitement and inspiration as I read. A new direction or challenge began to form for me of how to engage with the critical 'voice' of my revered former teacher while embodying the generous acknowledgement of my encouraging colleague. I laughed as a strange image came to mind of their merger as well as a recognition that trying to appreciate their different perspectives could move us to new possibilities.

Closing the circle

If I (Jo) return now to the image of the sheet of paper that my 'felt sense' offered to me, and my focusing and breathing smoothed and opened out for me as I started this chapter, what do I see? I see a sheet of paper richly written with the ideas of the contributors to Part II of the book and all the possibilities those ideas hold for me. I will fold that sheet of paper carefully and carry it with me, with gratitude to these authors.

We rush between meetings, seeing families, dealing with email, writing reports, supervision sessions . . . all without taking time to 'close a window', shut out distractions, breathe and smooth ourselves out so that we can be fully open to what it is we are doing in the moment. If this experience resonates with you, our reader, like us, you might try integrating the practices offered by the authors of Part II into your working lives.

References

Weingarten, K. (2003) *Common Shock – Witnessing Violence Every Day: How we are Harmed, How we can Heal*. New York: Dutton.

Weingarten, K. (2010) Reasonable hope: construct, clinical applications, and supports. *Family Process*, 49(1), 5–25.

12 After words

Our expressive bodies

John Shotter

> We are concentrating, not on the words 'good' or 'beautiful', which are entirely uncharacteristic, generally just subject and predicate ('This is beautiful'), *but on the occasions on which they are said* – on the enormously complicated situation in which the aesthetic expression has a place, in which the expression itself has almost a negligible place.
>
> (Wittgenstein, 1966: 2, my italics)

> What is happening now has significance – in these surroundings. The surroundings give it its importance . . . (A smiling mouth *smiles* only in a human face.)
>
> (Wittgenstein, 1953: 583)

We are creatures of our surroundings, and we adapt ourselves to the prevailing winds blowing within the social weather of our times.

Bending Trees

In Great Britain in particular, in my young days, having a 'stiff upper lip' was the 'order of the day'; displaying fortitude in the face of adversity, 'making the best of it', 'and exercising great self-restraint in the expression of feelings', were all a part, then, of 'being a man' (that women were 'the weaker sex', was, of course, taken for granted). Rudyard Kipling's *If—* was still often quoted. Big boys don't cry. Indeed, as living beings, continually responsive in our bodily activities to events occurring around us, it is remarkable the degree to which we – by learning to control our otherwise spontaneous *impulses* to act – 'tailor' our expressive bodily activities to fit the social requirements of our circumstances. Well-educated people are expected to be 'coolly rational' – and this, of course, can show up only too easily in those of us attempting, as professionals, to understand better the working of psychotherapeutic processes.

But currently, a whole new landscape of concerns seems to be gradually coming over the horizon amongst those of us with a professional interest in people's relations with each other and with their surroundings. A shift, a major shift, is beginning to take place in how we think and talk in relation to our communication with each other, and it is reflected in all the concerns voiced by the contributors to this book. As Jo Bownas says in the Introduction to this book (p. 2):

> I had lots of ways of inviting trainees to reflect on and elaborate their use of language, but a limited repertoire of ways to explore and address how they were experiencing, thinking about and using their bodies when practising therapy.

While Glenda Fredman notes in her chapter 5 (p. 65):

> Words are not only heard or received but they also move the talker. These movements can be seen and felt by the listener who, in turn, is moved: we touch each other and our selves with our expressions and the words we speak move both our selves and others to different positions.

Which, of course, reminds me of Tom Andersen's (1996: 121) words:

> Spoken words and bodily activity come together in a unity and cannot be separated . . . The listener who sees as much as he or she hears will notice that various spoken words 'touch' the speaker differently. The speaker is touched by the words as they reach his or her own ears. Some words touch the speaker in such a way that the listener can see him or her being moved.

These words are clearly *special* words for that speaker. *More* than merely 'information transmission' is occurring here. It is that '*more*' that we need to bring to light, as all the writers in this book realise.

Let me list a few of the shifts in our concerns as they immediately occur to me: expressive communication is not just the provision of informative language; feelings are prior to ideas; bodies not heads; what we just do spontaneously is more important than what we do deliberately; what just *happens* to us over and above our wanting and doing (Gadamer, 2000: xxviii); *similarities* and *likenesses* (metaphors and images) along with *differences* are more basic than *exact samenesses* (correspondence with theories or models); we need to attend to languaged-activities not just to language *and* activities; listening is more important than speaking; worrying about 'where next?' (the future) concerns us more than 'why now?' (the past); ordinary words (down on the ground) matter, technical terms (up in the air) confuse; noticing reactions is more important than searching for diagnostic symptoms – all in all, the fact is, we are more creatures of our contexts, of our occasions, of our meetings, than of our ideas, beliefs and assumptions. As John Cromby notes (2015: 1), 'before anything else we are feeling bodies'. Like the trees in the picture, growing up in a prevailing wind near the sea, we grow in relation to it. In short, we are more like plants than computers.

So how should supervisors, those training anxious young therapists in how to approach people in mental distress needing help, approach their trainees? As being like apprentice mechanics learning to *repair* the mechanisms 'making people tick' (horrible expression!); or like gardeners attentive to the social 'soil' and social 'wind' and 'sun' conducive to a person's further growth and development? The answer is clear. Consequently, we should ask not what is going on inside a person's head, but what have their heads 'gone on' inside of, and what are they still 'going on inside of'. For again, as Glenda Fredman notes in her chapter, how we are 'placed' or 'positioned' in relation to all else in our surroundings exerts a powerful influence on the 'openings' for the next steps forward we feel are available to us.

Also, as Jo and Glenda note, it is 'Systemic therapists like James Griffith and Melissa Elliot Griffith (1994) and Tom Andersen (1998) [who have] brought the body back into focus in systemic therapy with clients' (p. 2), and in a moment I would like to say something about them both. But first, let me note, it was a just a little phrase of Vygotsky's (1962: 90) that started me off:

> . . . consciousness and control only appear at a late stage in the development of a function, after it has been used and practiced unconsciously and spontaneously. In order to subject a function to intellectual and volitional control, we must first possess it.

In other words, the spontaneous responsiveness of our living bodies to events occurring around us, 'call' responses out of us, whether we like it or not, and these 'condition', so to speak, what later we can bring ourselves to do under our own direction. Thus, in that sense, it is not going too far to say: our activities shape our brain (or our mentalities) at least as much, if not more, than our brains shape our activities. To build up some new potentialities within ourselves, we need first to submit ourselves to some new experiences, to put ourselves (or be put) into some new surroundings.

Another little bit of Vygotsky (1962: 56) was also important to me: 'All the higher psychic processes are mediated processes, and signs are the basic means used to master and direct them', he said, '. . . that sign is the *word*, which at first *plays the role of means* in forming the concept and later becomes its symbol' (my italics). The bodily expressed words, people's utterances, play the role of *means* in the way in which they express them: with emphasis, along with facial expressions and tones of voice; with a certain bodily posture; finger pointings; eye contact; smiles; frowns, etc. – and above all, all timed, or 'orchestrated', in response to how we notice our children responding in their turn. Each different expression 'calling out' a different response from us. Thus it is that we are helped, as children, to focus our attention, to pick out distinctive features, to make connections, and in general *to relate ourselves* to the others and 'othernesses' in our otherwise somewhat bewildering surroundings in a very particular way – the *way* those in our culture *do it*!

But this radical process of coming *to master and direct* (Vygotsky) our own spontaneous responses to events, to direct what begins within us simply as a *particular movement of bodily feeling* in such a way as to maintain our 'coolly rational' attitude to life, can, as Griffith and Elliott Griffith (1994) illustrate, sometimes have some deeply grave, but utterly astonishing *somatic* consequences. For instance, a man, Mr Duquesnay, finally hospitalised after having been treated in an epilepsy clinic for two years, began to be seen by Jim Griffith and Melissa Elliott Griffith when his seizures were finally diagnosed as *pseudo-seizures*, as not truly epileptic seizures.

Gradually, as his feelings were explored in a setting along with his wife, after a number of sessions, it began to emerge that the family was planning to move to a new town, Natchez, where, as a boy, his father had badly beaten up the father of another boy who had attacked him, and his family had to wait for over a year to learn whether his father would be imprisoned. Mr Duquesnay faced, as the Griffiths called it, an 'unspeakable dilemma . . . in deciding to move or not move to Natchez, [he] would either betray himself or betray his wife, but could speak with neither her nor with his children about the dilemma, lest he burden them' (p. 110) – his seizures were the result. When 'one cannot *not* perform socially – when performance is forbidden – one offers a somatised expression by the body as the *performance of a dilemma*' (p. 61). Our living bodies *compensate* as best they can for the upsets they suffer.

Perhaps a lesson that we need to draw from this case, though, is that *words still matter* – but it is *in their relation to people's feelings* that their mattering matters. And as we saw with Tom Andersen's words (p. 155), it is the special feelings that go into shaping how certain words are uttered that we need to focus on, that we need to notice. But we also need to understand another special 'moving' quality of words: as Bakhtin (1981: 280) puts it, they are

> oriented toward a future answer-word . . . Forming itself in an atmosphere of the already spoken, the word is at the same time determined by *that which has not yet been said but which is needed and in fact anticipated by the answering word.*
>
> (my emphasis)

In 'directing' us toward anticipating *this* future, rather than *that one*, our words can exert both an *ethical* and a *political* influence, not only upon how we treat others, but upon how we treat ourselves.

In the psychotherapy world, Tom Andersen (2012) has been one of the most influential people in bringing attention to our bodily activities. But this is because, as he himself points out, he was deeply influenced by a physiotherapist, a woman called Aadel Bülow-Hansen, who died in 2001, 95 years old. Having noticed earlier and worried that sometimes his talk 'froze' his clients, shut down their liveliness – his questions were *too unusual* – he was intrigued to find that she opened up her clients' liveliness, their bodily stiffness, by causing them pain:

> She grabbed a muscle, for instance in the arm, or in the cuff of the leg. When she grabbed that muscle, it produced pain. The body responds automatically with an inhalation, and when we inhale, we tend to stretch more . . . When the chest is filled and the air goes, for instance with a sigh, some of the tension in the body disappears.
>
> (p. 21)

The lesson Tom Andersen learnt from this was that 'a change is made by a change' (p. 23). Clients who found it difficult to get themselves out of their own mentally distressing problems, because their own 'answers to the questions contributed to the problem' (pp. 19–20), needed to be 'startled' into seeing the questions confronting then differently. What was needed was a new, *less usual, but not too unusual* question – like the strong, but not too strong grip of Aadel Bülow-Hansen: 'Her eyes told her hands how to work', said Tom,

> . . . If her hand was too soft, no change in the movement of the chest occurred . . . If her hand was too tough, or kept on too long, people made a big inhalation and did not let it go again. That was what she was looking for all the time. If the movement of the chest stopped, she immediately let her hand go.
>
> (pp. 22–3)

Less usual questions, while not exactly causing pain, can cause a 'startling' moment of *disorientation*, and the *necessity* for the client to search for a less than usual *answer*; questions like: *'When your hand is on its way to hit, if that hand could stop and talk, what would the words be?'* that Tom Andersen asked a man who had hit both his wife and his son. The man did not understand the question so this *unusual* question had to be repeated several times until eventually the man said, 'Stop what you are doing because that is not what you shall do.' When Tom Andersen asked, 'And, how would you say it?' he again needed much time and this question was repeated even more until he said, 'I will say it clearly . . . calmly . . . with conviction' (Andersen, 2008). The question took the man back into the moment of hitting, but now in a larger social context, a context with which he became socially accountable to himself for his conduct.

It is this continuous 'in-touchness' – the undertaking of 'a shared feeling voyage', as Daniel Stern (2004: 172) calls it – and the sudden *less than usual* questioning, that can 'startle' clients into seeing the questions confronting them differently, when their own answers were contributing to the problem. 'Shared feeling voyages', says Stern (2004):

> are one of life's most startling yet normal events, capable of altering our world step by step or in one leap. One major difficulty in grasping the concept is that explicit content must momentarily be put aside and out of mind. Another is to stay focused on the temporal unfolding of feelings.
>
> (p. 173)

Like Aadel Bülow-Hansen, we must let our eyes and ears tell our mouths and the rest of our bodies what to do.

All of these *reorientations* in how we think about overcoming the difficulties we face in our lives – many of them exact *reversals* of what we have always believed is needed in helping people to solve the problems they face in their lives – are the task of the psychotherapy supervisor today. Anxious novice therapists need help in developing, like a gardener's 'green fingers', the capacities and sensitivities needed to help 'place' a living being to flourish and grow within whatever surroundings they find themselves. This book opens a door into a whole, big new landscape of possibilities for the future. I have just picked out some of the issues that have particularly fascinated me over the years. We pick out and organise bits and pieces here and there, of course, in terms of our overall end in view; and, for me, that has been always to try and let the frontline voices of ordinary people be heard, not the experts in some office block at the centre of things, for they are the ones at the edge of where all new developments are in fact occurring. And Jo Bownas and Glenda Fredman, and all the writers they have recruited and united together to produce this book, have opened this new door into the future for us all.

References

Andersen, T. (1996) Language is not innocent. In F. W. Kaslow (ed.). *Handbook of Relational Diagnosis and Dysfunctional Family Patterns*. New York: John Wiley.

Andersen, T. (1998) One sentence of five lines about creating meaning. *Human Systems: The Journal of Systemic Consultation and Management*, 9, 73–80.

Andersen, T. (2008) Reflecting talks: my version. In K. Jordan (ed.). *The Quick Theory Reference Guide: A Resource for Expert and Novice Mental Health Professionals*. New York: Nova Publishers.

Andersen. T. (2012) Words – universes travelling by Tom Andersen. In T. Malinen, S. J. Cooper and F. N. Thomas (eds). *Masters of Narrative and Collaborative Therapies: The Voices of Andersen, Anderson, and White*. New York: Routledge.

Bakhtin, M. M. (1981) *The Dialogical Imagination*. In M. Holquist (ed.), trans. by C. Emerson and M. Holquist. Austin, TX: University of Texas Press.

Cromby, J. (2015) *Feeling Bodies: Embodying Psychology*. Basingstoke: Palgrave Macmillan.

Gadamer, H. G. (2000) *Truth and Method*. 2nd Revised Ed. Translated by J. Weinsheimer and D. G. Marshall. New York: Continuum.

Griffith, J. and Elliot Griffith, M. (1994) *The Body Speaks: Therapeutic Dialogues for Mind-Body Problems*. New York; Basic Books.

Stern, D. N. (2004) *The Present Moment: In Psychotherapy and Everyday Life*. New York: W. W. Norton & Co.

Vygotsky, L. S. (1962) *Thought and Language*. Edited and translated by E. Hanfmann and G. Vakar. Cambridge, MA: The MIT Press.

Wittgenstein, L. (1953) *Philosophical Investigations*. Translated by G. E. M. Anscombe. Oxford: Blackwell.

Wittgenstein, L. (1966) *Lectures and Conversations on Aesthetics, Psychology and Religious Belief*. Edited by Cyril Barrett. Oxford: Blackwell.

Index